THE TRUE
WORK
OF DYING

Dianne,

Bless you for all you give this world! You held Alex and her family gently in your heart and arms through a difficult time — Bless you!

Namasté,

Jan
xxoo

Diane —
your love, care
& compassion!
Heals us all!
♡ respect

THE TRUE
WORK
OF DYING

A PRACTICAL AND COMPASSIONATE
GUIDE TO EASING THE DYING PROCESS

Jan Selliken Bernard, RN, ND
and
Miriam Schneider, RN, CRNH

AVON BOOKS ◆ NEW YORK

THE TRUE WORK OF DYING is an original publication of Avon Books. This work has never before appeared in book form.

AVON BOOKS
A division of
The Hearst Corporation
1350 Avenue of the Americas
New York, New York 10019

Copyright © 1996 by Angels' Work
Author photograph copyright © 1996 by John Bernard
Interior design by Rhea Braunstein/RB Design
Published by arrangement with Angels' Work
Library of Congress Catalog Card Number: 96-33886
ISBN: 0-380-97329-4

Library of Congress Cataloging in Publication Data:
Schneider, Miriam, 1949–
    The True Work of Dying : a practical and compassionate guide to easing the dying process / Miriam Schneider and Jan Selliken Bernard.
       p.   cm.
Includes bibliographical references and index.
1. Death—Psychological aspects. 2. Terminally ill—Psychology. 3. Terminally ill—Counseling of. 4. Hospices (Terminal care)—Psychological aspects. 5. Hospice care—Religious aspects. I. Bernard, Jan Selliken, 1956–   . II. Title.
BF789.D4S335   1996   96-33886
155.9'37—dc20   CIP

First Avon Books Hardcover Printing: September 1996

AVON TRADEMARK REG. U.S. PAT. OFF. AND IN OTHER COUNTRIES, MARCA REGISTRADA, HECHO EN U.S.A.

Printed in the U.S.A.

FIRST EDITION

QPM   10 9 8 7 6 5 4 3 2 1

*Jan dedicates this book to all who have invited her
into the intimate moments of their births and deaths.*

*Miriam dedicates this book to the Immaculate Heart of
Mary and the Sacred Heart of Jesus.*

Acknowledgments

Writing this book has been a rich and difficult process of giving birth. As we have experienced the labor pains, many have served as our midwives. We give thanks to each of you.

To our families for their love and support;

To our literary agent, Neal, who balanced hard work with love and laughter;

To our typist, Carol, who never once complained about last-minute changes;

To the women and men of Providence A.N.G.E.L.S. Support Group for your courage and honesty;

To our editor, Charlotte, for her understanding and skillfulness;

To Dr. Bernie Siegel for his unending guidance;

To the staff of Visiting Nurses Hospice team who were our cheerleaders;

To the staff of Hospice House where our vision of Angels' Work was born;

To the community of the National College of Naturopathic Medicine;

To all those who have courageously shared their stories in these pages;

And most importantly to all our angel spirits and their caregivers who taught us what really needed to be written on these pages.

Acknowledgments are made to the following for their permission to reprint from copyrighted materials:

"The Midwives" from *Yellow* by Anne Pitkin, copyright © 1989, reprinted by permission of the Arrowhead Press.

"The Weaver" by Janet Peterson, copyright © 1990, reprinted by permission of Janet Peterson.

"Take Your Time" by Marie Eaton, copyright © 1987, reprinted by permission of Marie Eaton.

"Precious Stone" by Kathleen Fallon, copyright © 1994, reprinted by permission of Kathleen Fallon.

"You're an Angel Now" by Patti Meyer, copyright © 1992, reprinted by permission of Patti Meyer.

"We Won't Forget" by Nan Collie, copyright © 1995, reprinted by permission of Nan Collie.

"For Ruth" by Jan Selliken Bernard, copyright © 1993, reprinted by permission of Jan Selliken Bernard.

"The Story of Robby" by Jane Selby, copyright © 1996, reprinted by permission of Jane Selby.

"What Will Be Tomorrow?" from *Life Poems* by Tim Zoebelien, copyright © 1996, reprinted by permission of Tim Zoebelien.

Stories by Father Bruce Cwiekowski, copyright © 1996, reprinted by permission of Father Bruce Cwiekowski.

"My Sister Katie's Transition" by Evelyn Rogers (MEI), copyright © 1996, reprinted by permission of Evelyn Rogers.

"Don's Angel Story" by Georgeene Young and family, copyright © 1996, reprinted by permission of Georgeene Young and family.

"Angel's Presents" and "When Dishes Done" by Sherry LiaBraaten, copyright © 1996, reprinted by permission of Sherry LiaBraaten.

"Mary's Angel Story" by Dolores Folio, copyright © 1996, reprinted by permission of Dolores Folio.

"Dennis" by Loreen Dawson, copyright © 1996, reprinted by permission of Loreen Dawson.

"Alexandra the Brave" by Regina and Cliff Ellis, copyright © 1996, reprinted by permission of Regina and Cliff Ellis.

"Shawn's Butterfly Story" by Rich Reid, copyright © 1992, reprinted by permission of Rich Reid.

"Valerie (on behalf of the Ricker Family)" by Valerie Ricker, copyright © 1996, reprinted by permission of Valerie Ricker.

"Going Home" by M. Buckley, copyright © 1996, reprinted by permission of M. Buckley.

Important:
Please Read

The information in this book is intended to increase your knowledge about the process of dying and by no means is intended to diagnose or treat an individual's health problems or ailments. The information given is not medical advice nor is it presented as a course of personalized treatment. There may be risks involved in connection with some of the remedies suggested in this book. Therefore, before starting any course of treatment, you should consult your own health care practitioner.

Foreword

by Bernie S. Siegel, M.D.,

author of *Love, Medicine & Miracles*

There are many things in our society that we do not talk about. One of them is death. When I taught a course at a local college recently, the textbook contained two pages of terms we use to say someone is dead without using the actual word *dead*. For example, at Yale people don't die, they "Brady." That's the name of the building that contains the morgue.

Death is inevitable. Sorry to have to tell you that. What I find hard is living, not dying; what we all need to learn is how to live. Yet if that is true, why do we need a handbook for dying? The simple truth is that it's necessary because if you have not lived your life and you are not the keeper of your zoo, you will find it hard to die also. You will feel like you are failing everyone and be more likely to die at 2 A.M. alone in your hospital room.

Why at 2 A.M.? Because the doctor isn't there to stop you, and your family isn't there to say, "Don't die."

If you stop eating and switch to water, sipping only when thirsty, you will die in a few weeks. It is not a painful or difficult death. So if you meet someone who is having difficulty dying, it usually means that there is some conflict in their life that needs to be resolved before they go.

I have experienced the kind of transcendence that Miriam and Jan are sharing in their beautiful book. I have experienced it with my patients. Of course, there was grief, too, but we can learn how to express it and heal. This emotional healing process is something I must say we physicians need to experience as part of our training so we do not all act like we are suffering from post-traumatic stress disorder or feel that we are failures when we can't cure every disease.

This book will help you to understand that each life is like a candle. There is a time to burn brightly and fully until the last moment. Then you burn up, and your life candle is no more. What I hope you will do is exactly that—live fully and not burn out before your time.

Please read this book with an open mind and open heart. Learn the place for love, faith, hope, and joy in the process of dying.

Let me close with a bit of humor. Why? Because I want you to appreciate that healthy humor is always appropriate. A man was waiting to die with great joy in his heart; he would finally meet Jesus. The doctor entered his room and announced to the children that he didn't think that their father would make it through the night. The man became so overjoyed that he recovered. The family then told the doctor if their father was going to die again, the doctor had better announce it in the hallway.

FOREWORD

Read on in this sensitive guidebook on a subject that is so important to all of us but has become an unnatural event as society has advanced technologically and regressed humanistically.

As Thornton Wilder has written, "There is a land of the living and a land of the dead and the bridge is love, the only survival, the only meaning." Read on and become immortal.

Peace,
Bernie S. Siegel, M.D.

Contents

CONTENTS

Introduction

As you read this, you may have just returned from a hospice where you visited your brother and brought him flowers. Or you might be sitting in the bed of an oncology ward, wondering about a recent change in symptoms and how to talk to the doctor about it. You might be a person with AIDS in the final stages of the disease or a spouse struggling with grief as you hold the hands of your loved one in a coma. If you yourself have begun the journey toward death, you may be terrified by the unknown and wondering if you will be able to handle the suffering. If you are a caregiver, you may feel powerless to offer true comfort. Whatever your situation, you may be feeling a wide gamut of emotions that can sometimes seem overwhelming. Life has been turned upside down.

This book is about the final weeks of a person's life. It is a space of time that can be lived by the dying and their caregivers in a manner that is not always possible in our normal day-to-day experience. Often people enter this journey with fear. The fear comes from many sources: from not knowing what to say, from memories of past deaths, from experiencing or witnessing intense pain or discomfort, or from fear of letting go of the familiar. All of these emotions add to the mystery that surrounds the dying process.

Whatever you are feeling during this challenging time, our hearts go out to you. Facing death, either one's own or a loved one's is one of the most difficult as well as one of the most ancient and sacred experiences in human life. Perhaps it is made more difficult because much of our modern society teaches us to avoid dealing with death at all costs. Those who practice medicine often see death as the greatest failure, as the sign that all hope is truly lost. You may even feel that beginning to think about preparing for the death of your loved one is a betrayal or a denial of all that makes his or her life so valuable. We, the authors of this book, have a very different vision to share with you.

Our purpose in writing this book is to provide a positive, practical book of solid guidance for the dying and their families and loved ones. (Although Chapter 6, "Rituals for Remembering," is addressed specifically to the family members or caregivers of the dying one, we have tried to write each chapter so that it has something to say to all parties in this process, especially the person who is dying.) In these pages, we will offer information on the myriad medical decisions caregivers face. We will talk about medications, treatment of pain (both conventional and naturopathic), and the physical stages through which the dying one progresses. We will also discuss how caregivers can create a comfortable environment for the dying, how to communicate effectively with hospice staff or other medical professionals, and how to settle upon measures that bring the most comfort.

More important than all this, at least in our view, is that we intend to provide a message of hope and spirituality for our readers. In our experience as hospice nurses, we have found that there is much more involved in preparing for death than signing forms and talking to doctors. A host of spiritual and emotional issues come to the fore during the dying process: the dying and their loved ones often unpack years of spiritual and emotional baggage in the space of a few months, weeks, or days. This process is normal but rarely without struggle or conflict. Yet when families and the dying one assume the true work of dying, real healing, in the profoundest sense of the word, is almost inevitable—though often not in a form that many are prepared for.

In this book, we discuss this preparation for death by you and your loved ones as a natural process. Most of us have come to accept the value of natural childbirth and childbirth preparation training, yet it may seem odd to think of preparing for a "natural" death. (We use the term *natural death* to describe a conscious, hopeful death, not necessarily a death without pain medication or other treatment.) Yet the emotional, spiritual, and psychological impacts on a family of the death and birth experiences are similar in their force and intensity. They can often overwhelm those who do not seek out support. We have found that the parallels between the birth and death experiences go even deeper; our friends and patients have taught us that the process of dying mirrors the process of childbirth in mysterious and powerful ways. The pains of dying can be seen as labor pains for the mysterious release of the spirit, much as labor in pregnancy prepares women for the miracle of birth. Most importantly, both experiences *can* be seen as joyous and miraculous. We will discuss more parallels in greater detail later in the book. The last weeks of life leading up to this miracle are a very special time; these weeks present an opportunity for spiritual growth that is rare and precious. We call supporters and caregivers who make the commitment to being present throughout this journey toward death "midwives to the dying." They have a role to play that is as important as the midwife at childbirth.

In the pages that follow, we will discuss our experiences and beliefs concerning the essential spirituality of the death experience. We believe that human beings are much more than physical bodies. This does not mean, however, that we will direct you to our own spiritual path. We will draw on the similarities of the major religions and traditions in the way they describe and sanctify the passage of death. But we hope we can communicate the true sacredness of this event most of all by allowing our patients, colleagues, and friends to tell you their stories in their own words (set off throughout the book). These stories contain within them the real message of this book.

Our teachers have been the dying and their families who have allowed us into these intimate moments of the final days. Our own personal grief and loss during and after the death of a patient has opened our hearts and our minds to the journey the caregivers walk as they tend to the dying one. We have found that there is a tremendous amount of knowledge available to assist another to die with dignity. This book shares some of that knowledge.

The Story of Angels' Work

We, the authors of this book, began our journey as advocates for the dying when we met in 1987 at a very special place called Hospice House. Hospice House, located in Portland, Oregon, was a twelve-bed freestanding facility that offered nurturing and care to those on the journey toward death. A nonprofit, nonsectarian operation, it was founded by Joan Buell and Kathie Weidkamp as an educational and counseling program staffed by trained patient care volunteers. Both registered nurses, we joined the staff after the facility opened the doors of its inpatient wing.

Jan came to Hospice House after a nine-year nursing practice in the areas of obstetrics and women's health. She continued to work with the dying after the closing of Hospice House in 1990. Jan received a doctorate of naturopathic medicine in 1996. Her practice blends traditional and nontraditional medicine. She serves as a midwife at birth and death.

Miriam's nursing practice has been a ten-year odyssey. She has held a number of positions, including an appointment as clinical nursing instructor with Oregon Health Sciences University and Linfield College School of Nursing, Portland, Oregon. Most of her past eight years have been focused on hospice care. In addition to her work in hospice at Providence Hospital and Hospice House, she is currently a community health nurse on a hospice team associated with the Legacy Visiting Nurse Association of Portland. She has also earned a national certificate in hospice nursing. Her career in hospice has been transformed into a life's ministry, and she bears witness to her faith through spiritual training and volunteer crisis support in addition to her job responsibilities.

The philosophy of care at Hospice House made a deep impression on both of us. It emphasized the individual's quality of life, emotional and physical comfort, and attention to loved ones during the final day, weeks, and months of life. Hospice care was hand tailored for each patient and family. Its mission statement read "to provide care to the person close to death in such a way as to control pain and other symptoms, to foster communication and spiritual growth, and to give that person's family the support they require." The hospice was temporarily closed in late 1990 but reopened its doors under a new name.

Having grown and learned together in our work at Hospice House, we formed our business partnership—Angels' Work—in 1989. Angels' Work has provided a vehicle for us to share our experiences and honor the dying process through one-on-one counseling, support groups, workshops, and lectures. Our mission is to provide support, guidance, and education for caregivers and those on the journey toward death; we seek to share a vision of the dying process in a way that opens the mind, heart, body, and spirit to an enrichment in faith, hope, love, peace, and joy. We endeavor to honor differences, provide a holistic approach to care, and to conduct our business with integrity, accountability, and discernment.

"Midwives to the Dying" was the name of our initial workshop, which first presented some of the basic ideas that have evolved into the concepts in this book. Our first clients were health professionals, others in the helping professions, families, and those who were dying. Looking back, we can find a common thread that united all these special people at our workshops: each sought to validate, witness, and support the natural process of dying. We all shared tears and laughter, and most importantly, each shared his or her pain. It is this pain that became the bond linking all our workshop participants. It was the sharing of sorrowful experiences as well as the joyous and glorious ones that has helped us to increase the scope and depth of our workshops. We began to realize that important work was being done at these gatherings and that others could use similar assistance and support in written form.

We wrote our first version of this book in 1991; it took nine months to be finished, and it was truly a labor of giving birth to something meaningful and new. As we wrote, we laughed and cried as we would during any workshop.

The response to our small, self-published book—also titled *Midwives to the Dying*—was beyond our expectations and confirmed that something like this was badly needed. Since first published in 1992, we have sold several thousand copies across the United States and Canada. It has been used in various colleges, hospice programs, hospitals, nursing homes, and by health care professionals and families experiencing this process with a loved one. Yet so much remained unsaid in our little book.

It just so happens that our current editor called with an offer to publish this revision on the day that voters in our home state of Oregon passed into law the idea of assisted suicide for the terminally ill. It is not our intention to judge those who advocate assisted suicide as a means of coping with the suffering of dying, but as we followed the news stories and spoke with our neighbors, we became convinced that many who supported the measure had not been exposed to an alternative vision of the dying process. The experience added a completely new dimension to the mission of Angels' Work; there seems to be an even larger need to bring the information in this book to as many people as possible. We believe anyone contemplating suicide should not consider it their only option to deal with the pain and difficulty of death. Any decision made without an understanding of the alternatives is by definition a limited decision. We will take the opportunity in the course of this book to examine more closely the concerns that may arise in taking life prematurely. Just as those who are born prematurely experience challenges, there are challenges for not only the dying one but for the family and loved ones who assist in suicide as well. Again, we must emphasize that it is not our intent to judge another's choice. It is our intention to examine that choice in the light of what we know about this profoundly healing, sacred time and to assist you in making an informed decision.

As you journey through the chapters of this book, it will be like creating a painting. Each step of the way you will gather new colors to paint with, new techniques to enhance your creation. When your painting is completed, there will be a portrait of a beautiful memory you helped to create. It is our hope that the moments we share will expand your ability to be present with the dying one. Perhaps you will leave the bedside of a dying person knowing that in some way you made a difference. This memory will be with you forever. It will be an anchor to hold onto as waves of grief begin when the one you love dies. It will be a sweet connection with the soul that continues to exist even though the physical body does not.

Jan:

It seems too often that many hospice patients' most profound questions come not as you *[the hospice nurse]* are sitting quietly with them, but rather as you are about to leave their room. It is usually the busiest time of your nursing shift when you feel as though you have the least amount of time. But in our hearts, these are the moments that we have come to value the most in our contacts with patients. There is always time for them.

My patient Jim and I often would sit together at night and talk about life and what this dying time meant to him. It was just as the sun was beginning to peek through the darkness one morning that he softly asked me this question as I was about to leave his room: "Have you been witness to any healing of patients with cancer?"

I turned from the door and shared with Jim that in hospice work with patients in the natural process of dying I have frequently witnessed something even more powerful than the curing of disease. In the final weeks of a patient's life, I saw the healing of sadness, the healing of regrets from unmet dreams, the healing of families too long apart, the healing that comes from words that took a lifetime to say, and the healing that only letting go brings.

1

Home Deathing and the Philosophy of Hospice

Most of us have heard of the home birthing movement. Many readers of this book will have been a part of this movement, whether consciously or not. Simply put, this movement seeks to restore dignity, intimacy, and sacredness to a life event that has come to be seen in the twentieth century as a mere medical procedure. While a home birth typically occurs within the physical home environment, the movement toward home births has had a far wider impact. Now, many hospitals try to re-create a home environment in an institutional setting through the addition of *birthing rooms* filled with color, comfortable furniture, even Jacuzzi hot tubs and space to allow family members to gather and experience the entire birth event. Some may choose to bring favorite music, food, and drink. Each birthing space becomes unique to a particular family and offers an alternative environment for those choosing to deliver outside of the home setting.

Just as a little bit of home has been brought to the birthing room, we believe medical institutions and families should make the same effort to bring "home" to the "deathing room," wherever it may be. In its strictest sense, a "home death," like a home birth, would occur in your home environment. As we will explain in this chapter, this is a real option for families: In 1994 alone, approximately 300,000 people died at home under hospice care (*Wall Street Journal*, 2/27/95, Section B, p. 1). Jacqueline Kennedy Onassis made headlines for choosing to leave her hospital to die at home. Of course, more is usually involved in creating a home space than tacking up some pictures and arranging flowers. The old adage "Home is where the heart is" still holds a great truth.

In the broadest sense, we each create a home by the way we live. This home is structured by our thoughts and feelings, our relationship with family, friends, and our community. The physical dwelling we call home is really just a symbol of the home we feel inside, but the physical space is important to us because we go home to be ourselves. It's the refuge from a world filled with demands for our time, energy, and resources. Creating a home means we have taken the time to fill the space with items that please us, meet our needs to live, and express who we are. Friends and loved ones are welcome to gather with us in our home. At times we allow ourselves to be alone there to relax and simply be. However we understand the word *home*, it is important for every human being to die within the safety and comfort of what home means to him or her.

Why is it so hard, then, for many of us to accept that a deathing room might be as important to the dying and their families as a birthing room would be? As of this writing, approximately 80 percent of Americans will still die in standard hospital accommodations. (*Wall Street Journal*, 2/27/95, Section B, p. 1). One of the readers of our earlier book has shared with us how painful it was for him to experience the death of his father from Alzheimer's disease on a crowded Veteran's Administration (V.A.) ward. He and his family did their best to create a feeling of home in the small space they shared with other patients, but something profound was missing. It never dawned on the family or the hospital staff that this man's father might deserve the dignity of dying in his own room.

In advocating a movement toward home deathing, we are not suggesting that people should try to go it alone without professional support. Death, like birth, often requires the assistance of others. In hospices around the world, the equivalents of deathing rooms are serving the dying with dignity; according to the National Hospice Organization, Inc. (NHO), more than 2,100 hospices existed in the United States alone in 1995. Recent changes in medical culture have combined the philosophy of hospice with the principles of home care and visiting nursing. The history of hospice, its beginnings, and its subsequent development in our country offer some important lessons in the proper care for the dying.

Origins of Hospice

We can look to the very origins of hospice in history to affirm our philosophy of care. Indeed, this history is the foundation upon which this book is built. A conscious attempt to care for and support the dying throughout time reflects strong respect for life in providing compassionate, competent care and creating an environment that emanates hope, faith, and love.

Early forms of hospice are found at the very beginning of civilization, although little distinction was likely to be made until the modern age between what we today call a *hospital* (providing primarily curative care) and a *hospice* (providing only palliative care and comfort). Most early societies and cultures seem to have had some consistent response to community members who were in need of all kinds of care. There was a recognition that a community had a responsibility to take care of the sick or needy. The manner in which each community chose to respond differed between various traditions and cultures, but the basic response was very often the same.

For example, facilities we might call hospices were found in India in the third century B.C. The researcher and author of the book *The Hospice Alternative*, Anne Munley, describes these institutions, built by King Asoka (273–232 B.C.): "The attendants were ordered to give gentle care to the sick, to furnish them with fresh fruits and vegetables, to prepare medicines, to give massages, and to keep their own persons clean. Hindu physicians . . . were required to take daily baths, keep their hair and nails short, wear white clothes, and promise that they would respect the confidence of their patients."

In ancient Egypt, places of rest were provided for the ill, where medications made from salt, honey, and water from a sacred spring were administered. According to Munley, "long hours of sunshine and sea air combined with pleasant vistas" were an important part of treatments.

From ancient times on, however, established religious communities became increasingly responsible for providing hospice care. Each of the major spiritual paths has a rich history of responding with compassionate care in tending to the needs of their neighbors. In the Muslim world, for instance, adherents of Islam saw it as their duty to be responsive to the sick and provided ample hospital accommodations.

The European hospices (almost exclusively Christian in origin) of the Middle Ages have traditionally been viewed by authorities such as Dr. Cicely Saunders, Dr. Elisabeth Kübler-Ross, and Sandol Stoddard as the forerunners of current-day hospice facilities. Hospices flourished during this period due to the continual flow of Christians to the Holy Land, which was conquered, regrettably, by brutal force during the Crusades. It is notable that when soldiers in the religious military orders that undertook the Crusades finished fighting, many of them undertook a peaceful life establishing hospices. Eventually they created a network of shelters for the care of sick and exhausted crusaders and pilgrims along all heavily traveled roads and significant river crossings on the way to Jerusalem. The Knights of Saint John of Jerusalem— still in existence today—became the most famous sponsor of hospitals. Other religious orders of various types sponsored hospices, such as the Hospice of Saint Mary Magdalene, which provided care for women and the poor. (Many children were born in these hospices.) What is striking to the current reader is the evident respect and tenderness with which hospice workers treated their guests. Hospitallers belonging to the Knights of Saint John, for instance, referred to their patients as "Our Lords the Sick." In the words of Anne Munley, hospice guests were "not mere cases . . . but beings entitled to love and respect."

After the religious military orders, hospices were

most commonly attached to monastic communities. These places were built on sites holding significant spiritual significance for the order. The Abbey of Saint Mary in Jerusalem is an example. Tradition holds it to have been built on the actual site where an angel announced the conception of Saint John the Baptist. This hospice was administered by a lay fraternity connected to the monastery.

Hospice in the Twentieth Century

The passage of several hundred years has not changed the basic focus of what hospice care should be. However, many of the laudable principles and practices of the medieval period were lost or forgotten in subsequent centuries. It took a resurgence of interest in hospice in England and subsequently in the United States in the 1960s to bring the tradition back to life in a nondenominational form.

The renaissance of hospice is due largely to the efforts of the English advocate Dr. Cicely Saunders. Her life story in itself illustrates how caring for the dying can completely transform one's life and give it a new direction. She began her work with the dying in the 1940s as a registered nurse and social worker. Through her experiences, she strived for a dream first discussed with one of her patients: they both envisioned a restful place where the dying could spend their final weeks or months. Over the period of nineteen years, Saunders managed to earn a medical degree, undertook extensive research in pain and symptom management, took on administrative functions, raised money, and eventually built a genuine hospice in London, England. Saint Christopher's Hospice opened in

1967 and continues to this day to provide care. According to several accounts, Saunders often said it was her spiritual foundation that allowed her to begin this revolutionary work. She encouraged others to find some form of spiritual sustenance in their lives. Saint Christopher's Hospice was built not only on a medical foundation but on a religious foundation as well.

Another woman who has had a great impact on the way we view hospice in the United States is the psychiatrist Elisabeth Kübler-Ross. Her book *On Death and Dying,* published in 1969, opened the eyes of the world to the emotional, psychological, and spiritual needs of the dying. Having arrived in the United States from Europe, she visited the hospital wards and homes of those who were dying. They were her teachers. From these experiences, she has built a legacy of teaching and writings about the stages of death and dying and the belief in life after death.

For almost thirty years, she has been involved in caring for dying adults and children. Dr. Kübler-Ross has stated, "My goal has been, and still is, to educate health-care professionals as well as clergy to become more familiar with the needs, concerns, fears, and anxieties of individuals (and their families) who face the end of their lives." She continues to build on this legacy today. Her early work with the dying has ultimately led her to a ministry for adults and children with AIDS.

Both Dr. Saunders and Dr. Kübler-Ross have responded with an extraordinary effort of devotion and commitment to create ways of attending to the suffering of those dying. They have inspired us to speak about the benefit of maintaining this approach. The focus (then and now) of hospice care is to create a loving environment to cherish, refresh, and honor the dying ones.

The Medicare Hospice Benefit of 1984

The model Dr. Saunders initiated at Saint Christopher's in England has become the blueprint for the delivery of care in the United States. The first hospice in the United States opened in Connecticut in 1974. The federal government's Medicare Hospice Benefit Program of 1984 is a primary example of how we have drawn on Dr. Saunders's work to improve our own national health care system. This federally funded program, providing a standard of hospice care for anyone eligible for Social Security Medicare, has influenced and accelerated the development of hospice in our country during the past decade. It has opened many eyes to the importance of hospice care; the administration of the benefit has been imitated by private insurance providers to follow in developing comparable programs for those under sixty-five. As a result, the availability of hospice care has expanded exponentially over the past decade. It is now available to the majority of the dying population in the United States. Significantly, the benefit provides assistance to those choosing to die at home, broadening the scope of care.

Dr. Saunders and her followers have recognized that every dying person will be unique in his or her needs and desires for care. Yet, it is safe to say that the dying have in common a limited number of differing needs that are possible to anticipate: the stages of death do have a universality, and there are only so many ways the dying body will manifest a need for comfort and support. The ability to define the range of needs of the dying has helped clarify the kind of services and disciplines required of health care. In most hospice care units, a multi-faceted team has evolved whose goal is to provide comfort and support at the time of dying. The team is typically made up of the dying one, family, caregivers, referring primary care physician, nurses, home health aides, physical therapists, occupational therapists, chaplains, volunteer staff, and social workers.

The Medicare Benefit outlines in a systematic way who can provide care, at what time, and in what way. The team members may provide services at the home of the client. Any number of alternative settings are also possible, including adult foster homes, skilled care facilities, freestanding hospice facilities, group homes, hospitals—even city streets if care involves the homeless.

The first priority of any hospice team is to alleviate physical, emotional, and spiritual distress. One person might only need to have a nurse come regularly to provide pain management. Another may need all members of the team to visit regularly. Medicare generally allows for flexibility in this regard.

Another facet of the Medicare program is to provide the patient with durable medical equipment such as oxygen, a hospital bed, a commode, and a wheelchair. Medications relating to the primary diagnosis and to provide comfort are also included.

All of these components make up a hospice team that is Medicare certified. With the concurrent advances in programs among private insurance providers, our nation has developed the ability to deliver hospice care in a standardized, cost-effective manner to bring the greatest benefit to the dying one.

The Referral

Entrance into a hospice program requires a physician referral, which can come about in several ways. The referral may be initiated by the physician who finds at some point in a person's treatment that curative treatment is no longer available for the patient's disease; the time has come to change the focus to comfort and support. The Medicare criteria governing admission to hospice care requires the physician to state a prognosis of six months or less of life expectancy. (Obviously, this is an educated guess only.) Any end-stage chronic illness can be referred to hospice care. Typically the physician will discuss the referral with the patient and those who are involved in his or her care. The physician will then contact the appropriate hospice team, and the admission process will begin. If the patient is in a hospital, the physician will contact a discharge planner, whose job is to assist with the transition of care.

Families or friends may be the ones to initiate discussion with the dying person about hospice care options. At times, it is the dying one who will determine he or she no longer desires curative treatment to be sought, and a request is made of the physician. Not everyone will choose to use a hospice program, however. Often, dying people will have in place everything they need to receive comfort and support measures. Some nursing homes, adult foster homes, religious communities, and private-sector facilities provide more than adequate care during this time. The quality of a person's death isn't necessarily diminished by not having a hospice team in attendance.

It is worthwhile to note that not everyone who is referred and admitted to a hospice program will remain in the program. Some leave because their condition stabilizes. For others, the dynamics between the team and family, friends, or patient are not helpful or therapeutic. This small percentage may choose one of the alternative care management scenarios mentioned earlier. Still others—including family members and physicians in addition to the dying one—may not wish to give up the option of curative treatment at any time. They choose to fight to stay alive until the very end. Each person's time and place of dying is unique to that individual.

The person with a life-challenging illness who is considering hospice care should ask some important questions:

1. Do I desire curative treatment to continue?
2. Do I believe the end of my life has come?
3. What treatments are of comfort and support to me?

Discussion of these questions in some form will occur during a hospice admission by either a medical social worker or registered nurse. The registered nurse or social worker should also offer a detailed description of the services the hospice team can provide for comfort and support at this time.

Several other considerations may be addressed during the admission, such as the measures to be taken should the patient's heartbeat or breathing suddenly stop. A form called a do-not-resuscitate (DNR) order can be filled out in case such a situation arises. This form is signed by the patient or health care representative, the physician (it is probably mailed, as most hospice admissions take place at home), and a witness (typically the nurse or social worker directing the admission).

The DNR form asks the patient to indicate his or her

desire to receive comfort measures (e.g., oxygen, pain medication), cardio-pulmonary resuscitation (CPR), atrial fibrillation (electric shocks to the heart via paddles placed on the chest), chemicals code (medications given to keep the heart functioning), and/or intubation (tubes placed in the lungs to receive oxygen mechanically) in the event of a medical emergency. The answers given create a guide for the hospice team. One person may be quite elderly and request no extraordinary life-sustaining measures. On her form, the no column would be checked for all measures except comfort/support. Another person may be physically feeling well and independent at the time of his admission. His answer might be yes to all areas. There may be responses such as "do only CPR and nothing else." What is important to note is that the desires and direction of the dying one or the one designated to make health care decisions are obtained.

Whether or not you are in hospice care, it is always helpful at the time you are actively dying if questions such as these have been anticipated and addressed. This makes some decisions at the end of life less traumatic and confusing. Of course, there are many more decisions to be made to prepare for the time of dying than can be included here. You are advised to discuss all that is possible in hospice care with a trained counselor at the earliest possible time.

Moving Past Fear

At a time when we have made so many medical advances, it is difficult to explain why so much of the population still dies without specialized care. Whether at a public or private level, it is clear that people need to become aware of the possibilities and options of caring for the dying. Honest, open discussion of the range of options—and the fears that may keep people away from discussing them—can allow anyone to discover and share ways to move beyond immobilization and helplessness. Fears start to lose their power when they are named.

The following story written by Miriam for a hospice newsletter points to the important role that hospice workers can play in a home death administered by Medicare. Most importantly, it shows how the availability of hospice enriches family life and all who are able to be present when a loved one dies.

Miriam:

I walked into Marie's room *(not her real name)* and immediately saw the change in her physical body. It had begun, the final labor of dying. Her body was so weak all she could do was stare straight ahead and breathe. I knew it took tremendous energy for her even to turn her head and look at me.

The time we had was precious for me because I was there to say good-bye to her. I had been coming to her home for a few months, walking that journey with her and her wonderful family, providing comfort and support in the ways that my experience and knowledge indicated. I was part of a team focused on that goal.

Over time, we brought in a walker, bathroom equipment, commode, hospital bed and medications to soothe and relax her labored breathing. One team member bathed and massaged Marie's ravaged body. Another taught and guided the family on measures important to keep her safe and to conserve energy. Most importantly we brought open, caring hearts to listen to Marie and her family as they experienced each day. We became part of their family and they, of ours.

I know we made a difference. We were told in many ways through their hugs, smiles, and tears. The sharing of their tears told me most. Tears are released when a person truly feels safe and cared for.

I shared my own tears that final day. I felt love and sorrow in my heart. I was ready to let Marie go, thankful that her time was drawing near. I was also going to miss her. I told her I could see her body was changing and that her physical death was nearing. I encouraged her to take her time and follow the light that was so clearly shining from her eyes. Her body seemed to emanate a flowing soft energy. I thanked her for allowing me to share this most intimate time.

I began assessing Marie's body. It was a familiar physical check that I do time and time again. It helps me determine what I need to bring in to continue to provide comfort and support. It also became a part of the way she chose to express her love to me.

I asked her to open her mouth. That simple act took her a minute to accomplish. She quietly focused with all the strength she had been using to breathe and opened her mouth for me. Not because she wanted or needed to, but because I asked her to.

I touched her face and told her it was not necessary for her to continue to keep her mouth open. She held it open for what seemed an eternity to me. Her determination was so intense. Her eyes were shining as she looked at me after closing her mouth. She never spoke a word during that visit, but I heard volumes. I kissed her gently on her head as I left. Marie died that night.

I share this story because the honoring of this process of dying brings many intangible gifts. It is easier to recognize the physical benefits in providing comfort and support to those on this journey. It is, however, the gifts of the spirit that bring the life-changing benefits.

Death comes to us all. The most remarkable deaths are those without fear. I did not detect any fear during my last visit with this extraordinary woman. She was at peace. There was little fear on the part of her family, though there was intense sorrow from knowing her death would come soon.

What makes this story even more remarkable is the fact that this dear woman and her family had come from a deep place of fear. They were all utterly exhausted and deeply concerned for her at the time they came to be cared for by the hospice team. They were unsure of being able to provide the quality of care they desired her to receive. I spent many of my earlier visits reassuring them, providing information, and helping them explore their feelings. I offered this support to empower them with the knowledge that they would be able to provide the care and support she required. This message also came consistently from each member of the hospice team.

I realize time and time again that I do not walk this journey alone. It is a team effort. I wish also to acknowledge the spirit that brought me to her home at just the "right" time. The spirit moved me to say the words of good-bye to her, which I needed to say then and she needed to hear then. I also know in the times I pray for her, she hears my prayers and remains close in my heart. I miss seeing her, but I would not exchange the sorrow of my loss for one

25

moment of the precious time that we shared. The memory of that time is a beacon of light for me. My light is growing because of all those whose deaths I have been so graciously invited to share. I will not have difficulty recognizing the light when it is time for me to leave my body.

I believe the hospice model has a great deal to teach us all. It honors the best of what family is and provides a guide for us to experience "family" on the deepest levels. The healing experienced is life changing for those I am caring for and for myself as well.

2

Spirituality and Death: The Essential Connection

I honor the place in you where the universe resides.
I honor the place in you of love, of light, of truth, of peace.
I honor the place within you where if you are in that place
in you and I am in that place in me we are one.
—ANCIENT SANSKRIT BLESSING

The stories included here about spiritual journeys of the dying and their families form the core of this book. All the details in these passages are true; whether a story is told by Jan or Miriam or by a caregiver or family member, we have asked permission of the subjects to include it here. In a sense, each death described in these pages has become more powerful through this generous sharing of private pain and joy. We feel these memories can provide a valuable perspective wherever we may be personally on the journey toward death. We learn, or perhaps just remember, how to live our lives to the fullest. The author Terry Tempest Williams, author of the lovely book *Refuge,* writes, "Story is ritualized language, the umbilical cord between past and future. Story is like the wind: It comes from a distant place, and we feel it."

We do not wish to present ourselves as "experts." We walk this journey with the dying one as invited guests. It is not our place to judge another's choices. However, time and again, we have been privileged to witness what can only be viewed as a spiritual awakening among the dying and their caregivers. Facing the most challenging moments of their lives, the dying show us the human possibilities in each of us. Death and dying by their very nature push everyone concerned toward spiritual discovery. As witnesses to this natural life event, we are invited to laugh, to cry, to risk being pushed past our comfort zones. By so doing, we awaken to the truth and light within each of our souls.

In our culture today we are witnessing the beginning of what can be called a *paradigm shift* concerning the dying process. A paradigm is a set of rules, mores, and attitudes (either explicit or implicit) that (1) defines boundaries of culture and consciousness and (2) dictates what must be done to stay within these boundaries. Changes in paradigms can trigger explosive growth. Think of how differently many of us today feel about the value and wisdom of Native American culture and tradition as compared to how our parents and grandparents probably felt. In past times, the dominant paradigm held that Native Americans were "savage" and that their culture was "inferior." Today, this view has, thankfully, changed, and we are more likely to respect and value and seek out the teachings of the first peoples on the Northern

American continent. We believe that a comparable change has begun in the ways our society understands the process of death. This change will continue into the twenty-first century.

For most of our scientific age, medical professionals have viewed death less as a natural life process and more as a feared enemy to be defeated at all costs. In a popular culture that values youth and "fast fixes" above all else, most of us are apt to view the "tragedy" of death with fear and resistance. Better then to think about it as little as possible. However, like the caterpillar waking from its cocoon, our society has begun to awaken to the ancient wisdom hidden in its soul. Rather than closing their eyes to the process of death, more and more people are opening their hearts to its lessons. You are participating in this shift by reading this book.

Despite our recent past, there has been a long period in human history during which death was much more likely to be viewed as a natural part of life. Because hospitals were not accessible to most people until his century, the home was the central place where the births and deaths that shaped a family history occurred. Children grew up knowing that both processes are essential parts of life. In fact, as recently as the late nineteenth century, it was customary in many parts of the United States for the entire family to pose at home for a photograph with the body of a recently deceased loved one.

As modern medical technology advanced, care of the dying moved increasingly from the home to the hospital. Along with advances in medical care, however, has come a cold, sterile environment that can exclude children and limit family time. The "problem" of death has become one for technicians and experts rather than family members to address together. Minutes after the moment of death transpires in most hospitals, the body is removed and all signs of the dying one's presence is erased. The family is not encouraged to gather and say good-bye in its own way. It is our strong belief that it is time to reintroduce the love of family and the power of the home—even if at times only symbolically—into the heart of the process of dying.

This new consciousness brings about a great responsibility. Though we want people to make informed choices about this natural process, these choices can bring with them fear and anxiety. To regard this process as more than just a physical experience is essential. For without the feeling of spiritual support and enrichment, the dying process can be very lonely and frightening. We believe spiritual care of the dying to be as essential as physical care and consider it the birthright of each human being.

In the process of dying, there are moments when the dying person's personal world is full of darkness. After a diagnosis of cancer, for example, one may feel he or she can look forward only to tragedy, loss, and sorrow. Others who are dying may feel as though they have somehow "failed."

Having faced these feelings, the dying one can teach us a great deal about the art of living until we die. We have found that the dying and their caregivers who have a spiritual discipline or a belief in something outside of themselves are most able to move past this darkness. It is striking how nearly all such patients say the same thing about how they cope with the process of illness and death when they reach this stage; each tells how he or she has learned to be grateful and value each moment and day, not worrying about tomorrow or yesterday. One mother wrote about her five-year-old daughter, Alexandra, and how the diagnosis of cancer had changed her idea about the future.

Regina:

Having a child who has been diagnosed with cancer has rearranged our priorities and ways of thinking. I no longer allow myself to dream about Alexandra's first day of kindergarten, her daddy coaching her soccer team, buying dresses, getting her ready for the prom, her wedding, or gently holding her newborn baby in her arms. Instead, I hold my focus steady on this day. Because on this very day, I can hear her laughter, enjoy brushing her soft, long hair, lie in our grass chasing clouds and planes with our eyes, cook our meals together side by side, and read or play with her brother, Zachary. The prospect of the future is too painful, terrifying, and infinite; whereas the present holds our laughter and lives together and intact as we once thought it would always be.

A great strength emerges from within each of us when we can move past our own limited perspective. Those who find some spiritual support seem most able to let go of fear and limitation and appreciate what is happening in the moment. We can find in this "now" a compassion and courage to face the darkness. Yet, it is from within that darkness that we truly are given the path to light.

Webster's New Reference Library defines *spirituality* as "attachment to all that feeds the soul." When we speak of spirituality, we speak of an inner fire. Through spiritual practices of prayer and meditation, we develop the ability to allow this inner flame to ignite all of our senses.

For the dying one, opening up to spirituality or the spiritual aspect of life may involve questioning the very foundation he or she has built her life on. This path may involve finding a sense of self-worth in the letting go of the self, hope in the knowledge of certain death, meaning and healing in the midst of pain and darkness. Often, this path may be made easier through the discovery or rediscovery of a traditional religion or practice, or it may simply be defined within the human heart.

Dr. Cicely Saunders, the British hospice pioneer, has spoken eloquently of the role spiritual belief plays in caring for the dying: "I have found it fascinating that every front-line, hands-on hospice worker I have spoken with . . . has volunteered a statement of faith, or a direct reference to the spiritual dimension of the work. . . . You really can't do this work and not believe in something."

A friend shared the following story with us:

> One evening the night nurse of a hospice team received a call to let hospice know of a patient's death. She expected the call as she had known the family for quite some time. Though she left immediately upon learning of the death, it took some time for her to reach the family's home. The front door opened, and a family member said, "We did just as you asked. All the furniture is moved out of the way. The funeral home people shouldn't have any difficulty moving Grandpa." Puzzled, the nurse asked the family when they believed she had asked them to move furniture.
>
> "It was your second call. Remember, you called right after we had hung up and told us it would be most helpful to move the furniture out of the way so that the stretcher could come in and out without any problem. You were right to suggest it; we finished just

as you came to the house. It was actually good to have something to keep us busy."

The curious part of this story is the fact that the nurse had not made a second call, nor had she requested that the family move any furniture. After inquiring at the office it was clear to the nurse no one had made any second call from the hospice. She discussed this curious event further with the family. The person who had received the call was certain that it was the familiar voice of the nurse who had hung up just seconds before. The family agreed that they had needed to focus on the practical activity of preparing the room as all were very distressed at the death of their loved one. They had always relied on this particular nurse to bring them a sense of calm.

The family and nurse decided it must have been an angel who provided the diversion this family needed so much. It was exactly the thing to help them make it through the difficult moments that follow a death.

It is sometimes easier to allow the gifts of the spirit into our lives within a framework or a tradition. This structure helps provide the specific discipline and rituals that define a person's relationship to his or her higher power. The Native American tribes developed a complex belief system involving ritual and prayer as a way to communicate with spiritual forces. Each Christian denomination teaches some variation of the belief in Christ as the touchstone of faith. Jews find special meaning in their covenant with God. Muslims hold Muhammad's messages to contain the core of their eternal beliefs. Each spiritual tradition can be identified with a core belief, the principle upon which the tradition is built. You *must* believe in something to follow a particular path. This is the under-pinning of all spiritual paths.

How is a spiritual framework built? Where do you find the bricks and mortar to begin the foundation?

Father Santan Pinto, a Roman Catholic priest, developed a spiritual formation program based on five spiritual principles. He explains these principles in his book, *Prayer in Your Life.* In our adaptation of these principles, we relate how (in hospice work) we are in a relationship with God. We do not suggest that Father Pinto's principles are the only choice. We use these principles as guidelines to understand dying and death as a spiritual experience. We personally believe that these five basic ideas are found within each of the major spiritual paths. Our words may differ from yours but they encompass a source outside of ourselves.

The first principle: *"Nothing happens accidentally but everything is gifted providentially."* In other words, there are no coincidences. It is our personal belief that God exists and is connected to our lives within a plan. Others might interpret this principle in a different way, much as the psychologist Carl Jung did in his study of synchronicity. He held that the meaning or significance that people attach to the occurrence of seemingly unrelated events provides a clue to the powers of the mind and spirit, whatever the cause of the events themselves. Certainly, it meant a great deal to the family in the previous story that the nurse on call when the family telephoned "happened" to be someone whom the family knew and trusted.

The second principle: *"Since everything is in the plan of God for you, everything has purpose."* Being able to accept the sacredness of each moment, each occurrence helps greatly in allowing one to accept not only the journey to death, but all the petty difficulties and frustrations we face in our lives. In the previous story, again, we see that moving the furniture had a purpose far beyond the simple clearing of a path.

The third principle: *"God created man and woman in His own image and likeness."* We are, therefore, beings of dignity. We believe in a God who values us, holds us in such high esteem as to create us in His image. Could we do any less in attending to each other's needs? We are able to express by our actions how we value one another. In the previous story, we can see how important it was for the family to maintain dignity for its grandpa. He would not need to be physically removed with any awkward pulling or tugging on his body. It would be done carefully and thoughtfully. This principle also points to the importance of acknowledging and supporting each life's passing.

The fourth principle: *"To the one who is given much, much will be expected."* People invariably remark of those doing hospice work, "I could never do what you do. How do you do it?" Our response is that we are sufficiently rewarded in our lives to be able to continue. Hospice work is difficult and complex. The challenges are even greater for one who provides twenty-four-hour, continuous care. What we are proposing in the following pages has to do with making an effort that may at times push us outside of our comfort zones. It isn't easy to care for and attend to the dying. It is, however, rewarding. We receive much grace and healing from our God. This family, in the previous story, was given much to sustain themselves and each other after their grandpa died. They were able to complete the work they had begun with a profound sense of connection to their God.

The fifth principle: *"God creates us as unique individu-*

als." We each need to know as we journey toward death how precious and irreplaceable we are: our body, soul, and spirit are distinct expressions of the creative energy of the universe. This idea confers great value to each who dies. It allows us to accept gifts of the spirit graciously because we know we are important. It means we deserve to be among family and at home—in whatever sense of the word is appropriate—when we die. This principle also confers the great responsibility to seek out and honor each life, even those it may be more convenient to ignore.

The Meaning of Angels

Miriam once worked in a hospice with a nurse who had the unusual concern that for more than a year no one for whom she provided care died while she was at work. (This would be a pretty amazing occurrence in any hospice where those who are dying come to spend their last hours to months of life!) It is especially curious as this nurse felt strongly that her main goal in working in hospice was to be with the dying at their moment of death. "But you know, they do say good-bye to me before they leave," she told Miriam. She went on to explain that many nights when she was asleep at home she would suddenly awaken. She would feel the presence of one of the people she knew. It was as if they had awakened her to say good-bye. She was never alarmed at these awakenings because they were accompanied with a sense of joy. Invariably, she would call work in the morning to ask if a particular person had died during the night, and the answer was always the same. The deaths had occurred at the exact hour of her being awakened.

Another nurse shared with us the experience of a

death of an elderly woman. The room was filling with family as they were notified she was approaching death. Everyone had arrived except for one grandson. This nurse noticed the woman's face light up as she looked up toward a corner of the ceiling. The woman motioned to the nurse to bend down. Her voice was but a whisper as she said to the nurse, "Can you see him? It's Jesus—he is so beautiful." As the woman took her last breath with those words, her long-awaited grandson arrived. The nurse who spoke of this memory had the same wonder and peace shining through her eyes as she had described in the story.

The experience of spiritual or other beings that only the dying person can see is a familiar theme. The presence may be a relative or friend who has died. There may be more than one person. The beings can be children, men, or women. The dying one may know them or not. For many, the most accurate description of these visits is an angelic presence. We believe the visits begin to prepare the dying one and those who care for him or her. The death moment is somehow fulfilled with the comings and goings of these heavenly visitors.

In order to discuss spiritual presences that we may be unable to discern with our earthly senses, we look once again to the rich history of religious teachings. Many paths teach of angels in some sense of the word, that is, purely spiritual beings who can communicate with us on a spiritual level. Angels have been described as being messengers, protectors, guardians, and helpers. Joan Webster Anderson, in her book *Where Angels Walk,* states that the ancient Hebrews believed "angels constitute the 'court of heaven.' " Many Christians believe God created angels before humans. Islam teaches much the same. The Hindu *Asparas* were angelic creatures. It is believed they would hold the deceased in their wings and carry them to paradise. In the *Yuwipi* ceremony of the Lakota Sioux, it is common for the medicine men to see and speak to spirits of the tribe's ancestors.

Miriam:

I am not sure when in my nursing career I became consciously aware that something or someone fills the room of the dying one. It is a profound presence. This awareness began to intensify after I attended several deaths. Initially, I began to recognize a change in the atmosphere upon entering the room of someone close to death. I had grown accustomed to the emotional and physical changes a person undergoes shortly before death. The spiritual changes were more subtle. I gradually recognized as I became quieter within my heart that the spiritual growth of someone close to death was obvious. In time I could simply walk past a room and sense these changes and how a body was close to death without directly perceiving the dying one's physical or emotional changes.

One night I went to provide nursing care to a man who had been with us for months. Walking down the hallway, I noticed a marvelous golden glow emanating from his room. My heart filled with a sense of peace upon entering; I had not expected this. It so overwhelmed me I simply stood in the middle of the room smiling and reveling in the peacefulness. This man I had spent so many nights caring for was quietly lying in his bed, his eyes closed. His skin was translucent, porcelainlike. I knew he would be dying soon and would die in peace. He died just hours after I had left. The nurse with him said she had just happened to come into his room as he was taking his last breaths. "It was so quick and quiet," she said.

Whatever your beliefs about angels, it is difficult to ignore the frequency with which they appear in accounts our clients and friends have shared with us. Angels and the belief in them serve an important role in the transitions of life. It is our belief that if we are spiritually present with others in a beneficial way at the time of death, there will be observable, recognizable manifestations of God. Some may be uncomfortable with using the angelic terminology to describe these manifestations; even so, it is difficult to deny the increase in feelings of faith, hope, and love and a palpable presence of peace and joy that commonly "visit" the dying and their loved ones near the time of death. At the very least, we feel that a discussion of angels helps us describe the fact that true goodness is clearly attainable for every soul when it matters most. In the atmosphere of humility and trust that proceed from such spiritual experiences, we are drawn to unity— and to building family and creating a home. The ultimate experience can be one of healing.

In the general sense, we don't use the word *angel* to describe only winged beings. We feel the term can apply to any person, young or old, living or dying, who is clearly infused with the love and purpose of the spirit. Many of us can have the privilege of being an angel to somebody in a moment of need. At such times, we are more than ourselves; we carry the forces of heaven with us.

There are some patients we think of as our special healing angels. One such man was Father Peter. He was a priest who was dying of AIDS. When he came to us, he taught every one near him important lessons. One night

Jan shared with him how impressed she was with his courage and openness about having AIDS. He looked up with those dying eyes and said, "How could I do anything else?"

A peaceful death is a glorious event. It is not always achieved, nor would we say it happens to only a few. It takes the effort of many people to support someone in an environment of peace. Some respond quickly to these efforts, whereas others resist to the end. The few who have complete peace in their death moment are usually the ones who teach us. They seem to be the ones who bring comfort to others even in their last breath.

Miriam:

Jan and I were first brought together by a very gentle, spiritual man named Stephen. He was only thirty-six years old, and he was dying of cancer. Jan would visit with him late at night. Though not many words were spoken, much love and healing was communicated between them, and they each learned the value of silence.

Stephen's disease had left him paralyzed on one side of his body. It was difficult for him to speak. Yet Jan felt that even when he was healthy he had communicated in a magical way without ever saying anything verbally. When Jan returned from a five-day trip, she phoned to see how he was doing. I updated her on Stephen's condition. I had also grown accustomed to the quiet, peaceful evenings spent caring for Stephen. It was difficult for me to receive Jan's call on the evening he died because I knew my time during Steve's last hours was to be shared with yet another loved one. Yet my possessive feelings left me the moment Jan arrived at the hospice and were replaced with a sense of the rightness of her presence.

Jan went into his room, and I followed minutes later. It was just the three of us in the room. The family had left for a dinner break. We had the time given us to provide comfort through therapeutic touch, a practice Stephen had always loved. Therapeutic touch, simply put, is a way to bring a calm, healing presence through "touching" another with hands from head to toe without making direct physical contact. We placed our hands four to six inches away from his body and asked permission from God to bring comfort. The energy between our hands, the body, and God's healing presence connects and eases the pain.

Standing on either side of Stephen, we proceeded after receiving his permission. It was the most glorious experience for us. Standing on his right side, I began to feel the presence of energy that emanated a sense of wholeness and well-being. Steve's disease had removed his ability to move or feel anything on that side of his body. By the time we had administered our healing touch from his head down to his toes, tears of joy were streaming from my eyes. I was able to stand at the foot of his bed and rejoice for him.

Jan:

I remained with Stephen after Miriam left. His breathing was labored and erratic, and he was very close to death. His face was so beautiful, radiant, and peaceful—no longer sad or pained. His body was stronger, moving toward the light, toward wholeness once again. Suddenly a vision came to me of a marathon runner. Steve had loved to run before he became sick. I told Steve what I was seeing, that this was his final race. The finish line was in sight, but it was his to cross, not mine. I coached him along as he ran faster and faster to the finish line. His face changed, and his breathing increased. His whole body seemed to tighten as he pushed his way across to win the race of his life, to be reborn. I had one hand on his abdomen and one on his head. Realizing he was close to death, I started to get up to call for his family. An extraordinary thing happened. My hands became like cement. I could not move them. Steve was very clearly telling me to stay and that this was how it should be.

As I held him closely, I felt his breath slow down and his heartbeat move into a different dance. He sighed a beautiful breath, and then as I looked at him, I saw the most incredible vision. He looked younger and healthy, and the sheen of pure ecstasy was present. I sat there in awe, crying, not because I was sad, but because I was so honored that he had chosen me to share this intimate rebirth. He honored me in a way I had never before been honored.

Miriam:

I returned to the room shortly after he died. The family gathered. The ritual of saying good-bye was completed. The night ended with me sitting alone in a chair after everyone had left. After hours full of activity, the quiet of this moment still lingers on in my memory. Just as I was remembering Steve's passage, I felt someone kiss me on the top of my head and a voice saying thank you and good-bye. I looked around somewhat startled. I thought I had been quite alone. Indeed, as I looked around, I could see nothing but the empty room.

SPIRITUALITY AND DEATH: THE ESSENTIAL CONNECTION

We intend to describe the many ways people spiritually attend to the dying throughout this book. These experiences will testify to the benefits received by everyone connected to the event. Our sharing in Stephen's death was a turning point for us. We built our business Angels' Work from that holy experience. It was no coincidence that the two of us had been called to be there, just as it was no coincidence that we both were involved in a disciplined nursing practice and both trained in therapeutic touch. This training and discipline allowed us to connect with God, ourselves, and another human being to comfort physically, emotionally, and spiritually. The experience manifested itself in an orderly, intentional way, which maintained the dignity of all present.

The measure of this transcendent death experience can be found in the growth of our personal spiritual journeys, the continuing development of our business to provide comfort and support to those throughout the dying process, and the immense healing we witness within and with others as we write this book. The fact that this book exists at all is due to these most extraordinary times of birth and death and the angels who have carried us through them. Our lives reflect an increase in faith, hope, and love because of these experiences. These are the rewards we value most.

Spiritual growth comes to those who attend to the dying. It comes in waves each person requires and at a pace that is consonant to their lives. It usually requires an intentional effort. How each of us measures this effort is unique. The special qualities each of us brings to the dying one are immensely important. We each bring a gift only possible for us to give.

The Strengthening of the Spirit

There is another common aspect of the spiritual experience of death: a desire in the dying and caregivers to enrich the death moment with a full appreciation of the value of life and its purpose. In the introduction of the book *Words to Love By ... Mother Teresa,* Frank J. Cunningham writes that "Mother Teresa of Calcutta has a dream—that before they die all people will know that they are loved. She devotes her life to making this dream a reality.... She tells a story of walking past an open drain and catching a glimpse of something moving in it. She investigated and found a dying man whom she took back to a home where he could die in love and peace.... " 'I live like an animal in the streets,' the man told her. 'Now I will die like an angel.' ... 'How wonderful to see a person die in love,' she exclaims, 'with the joy of love, the perfect peace of Christ on his face.' "

Mother Teresa has also said that those who come to help her in this work are not all Christians. It is her message that by assisting the dying the Hindus become better Hindus; the Catholics, better Catholics; Jews, better Jews. The point is, regardless of what the belief system a person may hold, there is a strengthening of belief.

We are seeing a resurgence of the search for spirituality. We all need a lifeline to pull us in and gently hold us. In hospice care we don't just attend to the body. We see the care of the spirit as an essential part of the whole. The whole of our humanity—physical, emotional, intellectual, social, and spiritual—is greater than the individual elements. The self includes both outer and inner aspects. It includes the body and the spirit, the mind and the heart.

SPIRITUALITY AND DEATH: THE ESSENTIAL CONNECTION

Whether you yourself are dying or you are assisting someone who is, it is important to ask what you consider holy or sacred. One family we cared for saw spirituality in the compassion given to their loved one by the hospice staff. For others it has been more defined through religious services, prayer, or meditation. For still others it has been found during walks in the woods. It is finding that quiet place inside of each of us that brings us back to center. For us, it is that place that brings us back to God.

Jan:

Nick did not believe in God, but he believed in a power outside of himself. He struggled with the whole concept of spirituality. Having been raised in a strict fundamentalist environment, he turned away from anything that was even remotely spiritual. Where he truly found spirit was when he would work in his garden. However, as his cancer advanced, it was no longer possible for him to perform physical labor. No longer did he have an outlet that helped him put the fire back in his soul. One night we brought pots, soil, and packets of seeds to a support group we were facilitating. Nick moved wholeheartedly into this project. We watched as he tenderly filled his pot with dirt and very mindfully planted each seed. We were witnessing a very sacred ritual. The seeds were placed an equal distance apart. The dirt was smoothed lovingly over each seed. He worked very quietly. His eyes were filled with peace. This planting ritual brought him back to his center and relit the fire of his spirit. Even as his physical body failed him, his spirit was fed each time he looked at his growing seeds.

In a research study done on the spiritual aspects of hospice care, nurse/teacher Anne Munley stated, "Hospice patients define spiritual support on three levels": (1) strength drawn from God; (2) strength generated by prayer seeking answers to questions of meaning and the acceptance of mortality; and (3) strength gleaned from caring relationships with staff and others.

For patients who claimed no specific religious beliefs, spirituality involved compassionate care and the acceptance of each person's personal beliefs. For patients whose spirituality was expressed in a specific religious practice, spiritual support involved the above levels as well as what Munley describes as "a willingness to enter into and appreciate a patient's experience of what he or she considers divine." For patients whose spirituality was a combination of "personal and institutional religion," it involved all of the above plus the availability of ceremonies and rituals that they found brought comfort and support.

Our hospice patients and their families teach us what courage and steadfastness are. Through the process of spiritual awakening, we are shown places in ourselves that we have not seen before. Within each of us is a source of great strength, compassion, and beauty. When we tap into this place, we are inspired to connect to others, give comfort, and support those around us, even in dark times.

Our lives are filled with many journeys. We cannot compare one person's journey to another. Whether our quest is a vision quest in the deep forests or the awakening to the darkness within ourselves, all have common threads. These journeys force us to pull on our inner resources of fire and light. To feel fear, self-doubt, and anger is a normal part of any challenging journey. We need to honor these feelings in the same way we honor the bliss within our hearts. Experiencing these difficult feelings will eventually bring us to our bliss.

Achieving Peace

When we feel difficult feelings, it is more important than ever to remember one's spiritual foundation. Often, the greatest service the caregiver can offer the dying one is a gentle reminder of that person's most cherished beliefs. We have found that directing or guiding people to rely on their spiritual source is an invaluable tool to provide a sense of peace and balance. Those who have been involved with a spiritual discipline will invariably begin to pray. People who do not have a tradition or prayer experience may simply begin to include activities that assist them to relax and bring order to their life. There are certainly those who do not have the ability to realize order or calm during a time of crisis. Yet even they may discover a way to peace that has eluded them for much of their lives.

Miriam:

I was called by another nurse one evening to visit a home where a woman named Martha was actively dying; the family had asked for assistance. I had met this woman a couple of weeks earlier. In our first meeting, she told me about the many changes that were occurring in her body. Weakness, fatigue, and pain were increasing. Her daughter, son-in-law, and partner of three years had been taking care of her. They, too, were exhausted. The area of greatest difficulty for them was Martha's reluctance to acknowledge the direction in which she was going: she was dying.

Martha had fought the cancer in her body for a number of years, and she was not willing to give up this fight even though the cancer had spread into other areas of her body. I recalled her struggle to walk into the living room to speak with me during that first visit. Each movement was slow and carefully assisted by her partner. He anxiously responded to her every request—"Pick my feet up . . . a drink of water . . . reposition my pillow." Every action she took required another's assistance.

During the first visit I also spent time speaking separately with Martha's daughter and son-in-law. They had moved into Martha's home with their six-month-old baby. "We have talked about everything else—her funeral, her will, no extraordinary life supports if her heart or lungs should stop, but nothing about what these changes happening now really mean." As we talked, they shared with me what they wanted to say to their mother.

It was providential that I was the nurse to return to Martha's home on the eve of her death a few days later. By then, numerous friends and family had gathered in the home. We all entered Martha's bedroom. She was sitting up, her breathing was labored. She struggled with each breath. Her brow was furrowed, every muscle in her body tightened to keep her upright. She was no longer able to speak to let us know what to do to comfort her.

I increased the pain medication, explaining to her and all present how this would relax her muscles in her body and also make breathing easier. Her family and I repositioned her on the bed until we could see

48

her facial expression relaxing, her breathing become less labored, and her body nestle into the pillows placed for comfort.

I took her hand and began to explain what I saw happening in her body. I gradually said the words that had been avoided for so long: she was dying. Stroking her hand, I listened to each family member gathered around her bed. There were at least eight present. They asked, "How do we keep her comfortable? What should we do? How long will this last? Should she go to the hospital?"

Martha's daughter was beside me as I explained to everyone that Martha was being wonderfully, lovingly, and competently cared for. The focus of her care would now be to keep her comfortable. I asked what Martha believed would happen to her when she died. Everyone spoke in turn. "She's going to be with Jesus." "Grandma and Grandpa and her brother will be there to greet her as she goes to heaven." Everyone had some vision to offer. I asked if there were spiritual books that mean a great deal to her. It seemed, again, each person knew something of the way Martha practiced her faith.

We spoke of the need to have one or two family members at a time in the room. A vigil schedule began to emerge as the family discussed who desired to stay. Many left the room and set up a space in the living room to gather as a group. Upon leaving the home, I could see and feel a noticeable change in the atmosphere. It was now quiet, peaceful, gentle, calm, and loving. There was no longer a surge of questions or concerns. Martha appeared serene as she lay in her bed surrounded by pillows, light covers, and the people she loved.

49

I discovered a few days later Martha died about six hours after I left. Her death was peaceful. She was never alone. Each member had had their time of quiet and prayer.

There are as many prayerful expressions available as there are of those who pray. The challenge continues to be to share in ways that promote peace. For some that may even mean not staying with the dying one.

Family members often ask us, How do I know what to say or do? What if I say the wrong thing? At a workshop presented by Elisabeth Kübler-Ross, she said she would share with us exactly what we needed to do to assist the dying. Needless to say, all of us sat at the edge of our seats, anticipating her magic answer. Her reply was simple: all you need to do is "shut up." Instead of giving us some detailed explanation of how to provide support, we received instead a pearl of wisdom that we consider each time we sit with the dying one. What more powerful spiritual support can we give than to sit quietly, lovingly, and compassionately at the dying one's bedside. We find it amazing: over and over again, if you just listen, the dying will speak deep spiritual truths. Each person comes with unique life experiences. Each brings personal spiritual truths.

At the same workshop, Dr. Kübler-Ross also brought up Carl Jung's idea that each human life is divided into four quadrants: spiritual, emotional, physical, and intellectual. In most cases, the dying person has a very developed spiritual quadrant. It is as if the walls we build around us in the normal course of life are not needed anymore, and they suddenly come tumbling down. Because the dying have let down these barriers, they are more in touch with spirit and truth. The light that they are reaching toward on their journey to death shines brightly long before they take their last breath.

As hospice nurses, we have often said we get to see the sweetest part of the dying person. The honesty that comes from within is astounding. How many times have we gone into a patient's room with our own hearts filled with sorrow and when asked how we are have said, "I'm fine." The amazing part is that the patient always knows you really are not.

Jan remembers one patient who called her to his bed late one night. He asked her, "How are you tonight?" Jan answered in the usual way.

He then said, "How are you really?" After Jan honestly shared her pain, he went on to tell her how he had lived much of his life in darkness. "I had money, power, and beautiful things, but now none of that matters. I can't take any of that with me. Now, when I am ready for more than material things, hungry for more intimacy—more of a spiritual connection—I am alone."

He wept for the years lost in a world of material goods, with little to feed his own soul. What a gift dying is if along the way you find your home again.

Hislop writes the words of spiritual teacher Baba:

> Let me tell you one thing: However you are, you are mine. I will not give you up. Wherever you are, you are near me; you cannot go beyond my reach. . . . Remember that with every step you are nearing God, and God, too, when you take one step toward him, takes ten toward you. There is no stopping place in this pilgrimage; it is one continuous journey, through tears and smiles, through death and birth, through tomb and womb. When the road ends, and the Goal

is gained, the pilgrim finds that he has traveled only from himself to himself, that the way was long and lonesome, but, the God that led him unto was all the while around him, with him, and beside him.

—SOGYAL RIMPOCHE,
The Tibetan Book of Living and Dying

We are proposing to each of you to reach out for that spiritual center not when you are dying, but now. The teacher and author Stephen Levine says it so beautifully: "If you are here now, you will be there then." Sogyal Rinpoche, a Buddhist meditation master and author of the book *The Tibetan Book of Living and Dying,* writes, "Believe as you sit by the dying person that you are sitting by someone who has the true potential to be a Buddha."

The Tibetan Book of the Dead is a book of Tibetan traditions that teaches us through prayer and meditation how to move into the dying moment fearlessly and compassionately. The following excerpt from *Padmasambhava* describes the death moment in the Buddhist tradition:

Now when the bardo of dying dawns upon me,
I will abandon all grasping, yearning, and attachment,
Enter undistracted into clear awareness of the teaching
And eject my consciousness into the space of unborn Rigpa;
As I leave this compound body of flesh and blood
I will know it to be a transitory illusion.

3

Birth/Death Parallels

The infant's first breath signifies and celebrates its passage into this world. It's the dying one's last breath that will mark the moment of death. Although the distance between these breaths may be great or small, these two breaths are far more similar than most of us would guess. It is our intention in this chapter to share with you the parallels between the experiences of birth and death. Through our continued work as nurses in the areas of hospice and obstetrics, we are continually awestruck at how these two processes mirror each other. In our hospice work, we have found that relating the birth event to the death event is a powerful way to make death less unknown and forbidding.

We are calling for a change in attitudes about death and dying. As we pointed out earlier, the prevailing attitude of many of us and much of the medical profession is to deny the reality of death until the very last minute. When there is a death in the family, often co-workers and neighbors may draw back, not knowing what to say. In most hospitals, the effort is made to remove the dying one's body as quickly and secretly as possible—and, we might add, without honor or dignity.

Just as we have rediscovered the holiness and joyfulness in the miracle of birth, it is time to find the same qualities in the "miracle" of death. They are there to be found if we will just look, if we will just remember what makes any birth special. The following sections identify the parallels between birth and death that have been shared with us by our patients and their families and the people from our workshops and from our own nursing observations.

The Natural Life Cycle

Each of our lives on earth is governed by the natural life cycle that exists for all humankind. This cycle begins with birth and ends with death. We speak of the need to return death into its rightful position in the life cycle.

From the moment of birth, we begin to deal with death. When we are born, the placenta that fed and nurtured us dies. In that same moment, life continues as the baby draws its first breath. The room is quiet as everyone begins to realize fully that a miracle has occurred. You hold in your arms a new life.

The mother experiences birth and death in the same moment of delivery. She may experience a deep sadness after the birth, a time of uncontrollable tears. Yet the next moment of holding this new life outside her womb brings a surge of joy to balance this profoundly intense experience.

Mother and child are not the only ones affected by

this event, of course; all those who are connected with them have had their lives permanently altered. The child is birthed into a home which includes family, friends, and community.

We base our discussion of birth and death on this understanding of what all of us have in common. We believe comfort and support are desired responses for all members of the dying one's family. We believe in incorporating the home and family into both processes in ways that are empowering.

Sharing the parallels between birth and death with the dying one and the family usually eases something within them. Most of us have strong, clear memories of the births of sons and daughters, brothers and sisters, or other family members. Of course, our bodies and spirits hold strong memories of our own births, although we may not be able to access them directly.

Our families prepare for death and birth in much the same way, and the labors of birth and death can be equally challenging and all-encompassing. Both processes involve physical, emotional, and spiritual changes. Both have sounds and smells that are unique. Both events elicit strong responses from all present.

Jan:

I had worked as a nurse in labor and delivery for nine years before becoming a staff nurse at Hospice House. Assisting with birth was as natural as breathing is to me, and I had never, never considered doing anything else. I would never have believed that I might also serve as a midwife to those who were dying. Then my friend Margaret told me about the opening of Hospice House, and something deep inside of me seemed to awaken. When I walked inside the door, I knew I had finally come home.

I remember so vividly my first night working at Hospice House. I was scared to death and so unsure of my skills in hospice care. When I met my first patient, Ellen, my breath was taken away by what I saw. She was standing by the window in her room, and for a moment, she looked like a woman at the end of her pregnancy. Her abdomen had begun to fill with fluid because of the cancer. Her breathing was very labored, and she was unable to bend over to pick up a card she had dropped. When our eyes met, I saw the same clarity in her eyes that I saw in women giving birth. It was a look that comes only from suffering. It seemed as though she could see into my very soul. I remembered what Elisabeth Kübler-Ross had said about being completely honest with your patients, so I shared with Ellen my fears, my uncertainty about caring for her. She smiled at me and said, "Come sit by me until I fall asleep." It was then that I moved from my head to my heart and followed her guidance about what to do rather than trying to figure it out on my own. I put a pillow under her back to relieve some of the abdominal pressure just as I had done when a woman was in labor. I lovingly stroked her head and hummed the song "Hush Little Baby" as she fell asleep. I still remember years later the feeling I experienced at her bedside. I had never in my life felt so at home as I did there at Hospice House.

Preparation

Discussing birth and death parallels is not possible without describing how the home is touched. A pregnant woman is noted for her "nesting instinct" before the arrival of a baby. When a woman and her partner are having a baby, much time is spent in preparation for the birth. Showers are given to honor the event; friends and families offer an endless stream of advice. The couple attend formal childbirth education classes to learn what to expect from the process in the belief that education removes some, though not all, of the fear surrounding the labor and birth.

The dying must prepare as well. The dying one needs others to help in a special effort to determine not only who will be caring for him or her, but also where the dying person will reside. It is through creating a safe place that the process of letting go is eased. The preparation for these life-changing events is critical. The quality of a person's death experience is directly related to the preparation of a home environment—no matter whether it is in a hospital, nursing home, adult foster facility, hospice house, or a family home. The physical space is not what creates a "home"; it is people that create it.

Miriam:

A woman and her husband emigrated from another country to the United States. They chose to open an adult foster home to earn their living. A man came to stay with them. He had no family, no wife, no children, no one except a friend to whom he gave power of attorney for his material needs. This friend came once or twice a year to visit and also took care of the man's financial needs. After two years, it was clear that this man was dying. He had spent his life traveling, fighting in World War II as a merchant marine, drinking heavily, and ultimately was dying from the cancer that grew in his body.

This woman who opened not only her home, but also her heart became this man's only family at the end of his life. The nurse from a hospice team came to this woman's home to share what comfort and support measures would be helpful to bring peace to his final hours and days. The woman said to the nurse, "I never planned to have him stay with me while he was dying. I always said I would not take care of someone at that time. Now that you have told me he is dying and how to keep him comfortable, I know I will be able to do this. I am his only family. He has lived such a hard life and has no one but us. I was not able to be with my mother when she died because we had left our homeland. Somehow having this man here is bringing back that sorrowful time for me. I can finish saying good-bye to her as I say good-bye to him."

Midwives Ease the Journey

We are using the words *home* and *family* in the highest sense. Those people who honor, respect, and allow the dying one's death to proceed with full support give a gift that cannot be measured by its value in dollars. Time and time again, families and friends speak in reverence of this experience of midwiving to the dying.

A woman who took care of her mother until she died made these comments to Miriam, who came to her home upon learning of the death:

"I was at work, but something inside me said I needed to get home. So I came home. It was just in time. My mom's breathing was different, her face was changing. I held her in my arms to get her head up higher. She died with me holding her. I can hardly believe it has happened. I remember her telling me of the time she was with her mother as she died. She held her, too." The nurse, who was listening intently to this amazing story of how several generations of mothers and daughters experienced birth and death together, each in their own turn, suddenly realized who else was standing in the bedroom next to the body. It was the granddaughter of the woman who had just died. Each woman stood in a circle in awe of the miracle of life and death and of the presence of generations of family past, present, and future.

The skill of midwiving may mean stepping back and getting in touch with past instincts and memories. As Elisabeth Kübler-Ross teaches, it involves listening and being attuned to the dying one. Being a midwife may mean being fully oneself.

Jan:

Ron had been in a coma for several days. I remember walking to his room at the hospice and seeing how exhausted the family was. The room was full of people, but no one was by Ron's bedside. His brother shared with me his fear of doing something that would hurt his brother. I asked him if he had been at the births of his children. He said he had and that they had been high points of his life. I asked him how he knew what his wife needed during that time. For a while he just sat quietly, remembering. "I just did what came naturally to me. I knew she didn't like me to hover around her but that she liked me to touch her forehead when she was not feeling well." I then asked him what his brother liked him to do for him when he didn't feel well. He said his brother hated how serious everyone had become since he was diagnosed with cancer. His brother always loved to laugh and kid around. "I guess he'd want the same thing here now." The family gathered around his bed, telling stories about the pranks that Ron had loved to play on people. The sadness was still there, but there was no longer discomfort in the sadness.

Is It Time Yet?

In our work we offer support and guidance on how to honor the death moment in the same way that we honor the birth moment. It is fear that keeps us from embracing death. This is a natural reaction to the unknown. Drawing out the parallels between birth and death allows light into the deep darkness, and brings something familiar to an unfamiliar experience.

A question that we are frequently asked is, When will the death happen; how much longer will it be? There is no one answer to this question because each person is unique. Each of us comes into the world with our own path to follow. We leave the world the same way.

"When am I going to die?" a patient once asked Miriam. She replied as quietly as he had asked, "You will be telling us before we can tell you." This is the only way we are able to respond to that much-asked question. We know each person's journey and time of death bring strong physical indications. It is clear when a person is in the active phase of dying. It is not clear how long they will need to be in that phase. Some enter quickly only to linger days beyond anyone can imagine a body to last. Others slowly let go, fighting with all their might to hold on to life. Some simply look you straight in the eye and tell you it will be less than a week before they will die.

We often compare the process of waiting for the death to happen to waiting for a birth to happen. A pregnant woman grows physically uncomfortable near the end of pregnancy. She becomes fatigued more easily, needs to rest more frequently, has more aches and pains as her body prepares for the birth, finds her appetite decreasing, and begins to put her life in order in preparation for this sacred event. Many times she will become more introspective, needing more support from those around her. Fear arises within her, wondering whether she can do this in a "good way." As her body grows larger with this new life, she becomes impatient. She asks her doctor, "When will this baby come? Why is it taking so long?" She goes to bed, sure that by morning the baby will be here. When morning comes, she is still as full of life in her womb as the night before. So she waits some more.

The dying one also has a preparation time. His mood is changing daily, each loss bringing him closer to the final breath. His appetite decreases; his pain increases; he has a strong need to be alone, to have people move slowly around him. We move back to our very beginnings. As infants we were loved and cared for unconditionally.

Jan:

A young woman was dying of cancer. Her mother was upset and exhausted and asked when I thought her death would come. For several days, Mary had been growing weaker but always seemed to rally back. I asked her mom what her labor and birth had been like when she was pregnant with Mary. She told us that she had had a lot of false labor. When the final labor did begin, it was a long, hard process. It took over thirty hours, and finally Mary was delivered by cesarean section because she was in a breech position. Even in the womb, she had been strong willed. As we talked more, the mother realized how Mary's birth process paralleled her dying process. When Mary moved into the active dying process, it took several more days. She waited until her birthday and then died at the exact moment of her birth.

The dying process has its own rhythm of care: repositioning a body through massage and gentle shifts, swabbing the mouth that is parched from lack of fluids, and holding and talking to the one you love as the body moves closer to death. The pregnant woman's body contracts to push the baby out of womb. In the labor of the dying one, the contractions are the progressive shutting down of the body, literally pushing the spirit out from within it. The body loses the ability to move. It can no longer regulate its own temperature. The ability to eat or drink is gone. A person can no longer do anything without help—except to leave the body.

Birth and death are both processes that need to be honored with respect and patience. Caregivers must have a basic understanding that it is the dying one's journey, just like the unborn child's journey. We must always ask, Am I serving the needs of the dying one or my own? We must always honor the dying one's privacy and needs. In the words of singer/songwriter Kathleen Fallon, who wrote this song for a friend diagnosed with cancer:

BIRTH/DEATH PARALLELS

PRECIOUS STONE

Flicker, see a flash of light
Quicker than the break of night
In a heartbeat we are changed
When a star meets the sky in flames

And we must/will hold each other
On this journey
Unpredicted, but not alone
And we must/will make a promise
In the daylight
That our love is a precious stone
A precious stone

Talking on the phone
Bad news found its way home
Now the cancer is ours to fight
Now more than ever
We look to the light

Like a diamond, so strong from the pressure of the ages
Clear with the wisdom sought by the sages
Forged in the earth with fire and ice
The rarer the gemstone
The dearer the price

North wind, blowing rain
Bending, we've learned its name
There's a storm now,
Here in our hearts
We will stand firm
We will do our part

Labor

The natural process of labor and birth is highly complex and mysterious. Each woman passes through recognizable stages as her body prepares to release the unborn child. Each stage is necessary for the preparation of birth. In the dying process, similar stages occur that correspond roughly to the labor of birth. The physical and spiritual body must pass through these stages to be released. In the next chapter, we will explore in detail the three stages of labor in dying: preactive, active, and death. It is appropriate here, however, to look at the similarities between the labors of birth and death.

In the labor of birth, the uterus contracts in response to a force deep inside the woman. There is uncertainty and pain but also a deep knowledge within the body about what it needs. As each contraction comes, it is like a wave of the ocean that has a beginning, a peak, and an ending. It demands conscious participation and a full awareness of the body and the soul. We must remember that each birth is a spiritual experience. In the book *Spiritual Midwivery,* author Ina Gaskin writes: "When a child is born, the entire universe has to shift and make room. Another entity capable of free will, and therefore capable of becoming God, has been born."

The labor of the dying is no less all consuming and demanding; it is marked by the same uncertainty and pain. Yet this process also holds within it the possibility of realizing and achieving the core needs of the dying. As in birth, there is a goal to be reached, to be longed for. The last thirty-six hours of Karla's life on earth recall a perfect memory depicting for us this labor of dying.

BIRTH/DEATH PARALLELS

Miriam:

I met Karla for the first time on a Thursday after-noon. She was thirty-two years old. Her mother, sister, and ex-husband were present. She was crying out and grasping for her mother, clinging to her and moaning for help. Her cry of anguish was "Don't leave me. Please help me." Standing next to her bedside, I could see a scared little girl wanting her mommy to protect her and make this awful time stop.

Her mother would jump up and race to her side. "I don't know what else to do. I sit and listen for her and then jump when she awakens. Her sounds are so loud, her breathing is so awful. It's not possible to sleep, yet I know I'm tired. My stomach hurts, my body aches. This all reminds me of when she was born. That took thirty-six hours," she said incredu-lously. "There seems little difference now. She had difficulty coming into the world. I guess it's going to be as hard going out."

"Yes," I said, "dying is very much like birthing. The labors of both can be very hard work, but those memories can help you to help her now." Both of us held Karla's hands.

I took the time to center myself in prayer, silently asking permission to attend to this family's needs at this moment. I realized then the angels were present. I did not see them with my eyes. I felt them with my heart. I can remember feeling immediately empow-ered and strong, with an intense sense of well-being.

The next moment I began to say, "You are doing wonderfully. This is very hard work, but you are doing it. You are not alone. Your family is with you, keeping you surrounded with love. You are safe." She

65

was receiving morphine continuously; I let her know I was giving her an increase of the medication to help make her breathing less labored and reduce the pain.

We sustained the effort to provide her a calm, loving space. By the end of the evening, she allowed us to move and turn her in bed without her screaming out in pain and fear. Her mother was at her bedside, able to speak to her calmly. Her sister kept close to her, offering wet swabs to moisten her mouth, holding her hand and talking with her. They managed to focus on this person they loved so dearly and what she was feeling. I stood watching a family administer love and comfort. I saw Karla appreciating this love and comfort. The process of letting go had begun.

The next evening, she was in the active phase of dying. Her mother was very tearful, but her fear had subsided. She knew her daughter would die soon. "Please stay with us through it. I have been working very hard with her today and need you here."

There continued to be a loving energy touching everyone who entered that room. Her friends came in twos now, giving the family time to go to dinner. Each couple spent time loving Karla in ways they always had. One massaged her, another put on music. They circled around her, speaking of the joyous memories they had. The energy in her body was decreasing. She was at peace. No more fear could be detected. She was surrounded in a loving light. Her friends left as the family returned.

As I was preparing to go to another room, I felt an uncontrollable urge to stay in Karla's room. Her body was very close to death. I told the family it was time. Her sister telephoned their father and other sister. She placed the telephone next to Karla's ear. Karla died listening to them saying good-bye. Her final breath was slow, quiet, peace filled.

Each woman and baby have a unique process of birth. Some births are short and intense, others are long. A baby may be birthed with a few pushes while others are born after long hours of pushing. It remains a mystery as to what determines when a baby is born and in what way. Each person present both at a birth or death experience have been invited to participate on some level by the mother or the dying one. It is vital we respect this invitation. We each carry our own energy, belief systems, hopes, and dreams into the experience, but we must always defer to the birthing or dying one's natural process. We must be clear about that from the very start. It is possible for the unconscious thoughts we carry into the room to slow down the dying or birthing process. Persons in the state of grace brought on by birth or death are very sensitive to all emotions around them. They are able to perceive things in an astounding way.

Jan:

I was invited to be present with dear friends whose baby boy had died while still in the womb. He was only seventeen weeks old when the angels called him home. The labor was difficult even with the support of many family members and friends. Not only was there physical pain, but emotional pain and intense grief as well.

My friend Rosie was becoming emotionally and physically drained. Near her bed was an altar with a picture of Mother Meera, one of Rosie and her husband Chris's spiritual teachers, with beautiful white roses around the foot of the altar. As the mountain of pain became more difficult to climb, they drew strength from Mother Meera. The labor pains continued for many hours. Rosie and Chris placed their hands over her womb and told their unborn child it was time to be born and that they loved him. All present encouraged him to follow the light. These incredible people who wanted this baby so much were giving his spirit permission to leave this earth.

As he emerged from the birth canal, still safe within his amniotic sac, a silence fell on the room. Each person there was a witness to birth and death in the same heartbeat. The amniotic sac was removed from around him. There lay this beautiful angel child with eyes of pure light and love. His body was perfectly formed. His spirit was felt so strongly as Rose wailed an incredible symphony of grief. What courage they both showed. More importantly what honesty I saw within them. I remember Rosie looking at me, and once again I saw her eyes filled with the clarity that only comes from deep pain. A part of her had died, and life would never be the same again.

I gathered the child's small body and placed him in our angel blanket and sang to him while I rocked him gently. Or did he rock me?

When a family experiences the death of a child, a part of them dies along with the baby. It is vital that we remember not the age of the body, but the age of the soul. Elisabeth Kübler-Ross has written a remarkable book called *A Letter to a Child with Cancer* in which she speaks to a ten-year-old who has asked her why children die. "It is like graduation," she explains. "When we have done all we were sent by God to do, we can return to our real home with God."

BIRTH/DEATH PARALLELS

Sounds and Smells

In birth and death, there are sounds and smells that are unfamiliar. There may be loud moans and sighs as the letting-go-of-life occurs. The body may also emit strong odors as it works to release the life inside. Those witnessing these primal sounds and smells may feel discomfort. If we move back to our own deep roots of birth, the sounds and smells can be like a poignant symphony.

Miriam:
I will always treasure my memory of Ruth. She was part of a loving family who all gathered at her side after she was admitted to Hospice House. The days and nights were spent together in saying goodbye. Her children, already grown, would gather and bring the grandchildren. There came a time when Ruth's children concluded their good-byes with a final remembrance ceremony. After sharing this ritual, each of her children had other obligations that took them away from Ruth's side. The day after they left, Ruth went into the active phase of dying. Ruth's oldest three grandchildren were notified.

Her granddaughter was the first to arrive. I entered the room with her while Ruth was laboring. Her breathing filled the room with an awful odor. Gently explaining to her granddaughter the changes that were occurring, I showed her what kind of touching would comfort Ruth. I sat by her bedside as the loving granddaughter shared her memories of Ruth while stroking her forehead softly and holding her hand.

A short time later, a grandson arrived. He was entering the room but stopped because the odor had increased in intensity. After placing a small fan on her bedside table, opening a window, and lighting some incense, the grandson was able to take his place at his grandmother's side. The three of them huddled close together. The grandchildren were stroking Ruth and sharing their love with her. The room was filled with a peaceful aura.

This third grandson arrived. It wasn't two minutes later when one of them came for me. I walked into the room and saw that Ruth had died. I exclaimed, "What a gift of love. She waited for all of you to come. You were the ones she invited to witness her departure."

Breath

Our breathing takes on a quality and rhythm unique to each moment in our lives. In birth, the amniotic fluid serves as our protector. The infant is content within the warmth of these waters. Rather than control his breathing, he trusts the life process and adapts. The dying one's lungs fill up with fluid as he moves closer to death. He must trust the process and release control of his breathing. In this drama, we are reminded of the origins of our humanity.

For the dying one, breathing changes from a regular rhythm to an erratic one. There may be times when suddenly you will not hear any breathing and wonder if death has come, but then moments later, the breathing will resume. We usually wait until the family notices the breathing has stopped before we say it. It is a way to let them recognize on their own that the death has occurred.

BIRTH/DEATH PARALLELS

Jan:

There was a couple who had been married for fifty-one years. The husband was dying and having a very hard time leaving his life partner. His breathing was very erratic, and there were long periods when he did not breathe. At one point, several minutes passed without any breaths. My friend Clare and I stayed quiet, waiting for the family to see that he had died. Suddenly he took in an enormous breath, like one you take when you have been under water for a very long time. I felt his spirit hovering around us, unsure of leaving this earth.

I shared with his wife that I thought perhaps he was worried about her and whether or not she would be OK. She leaned very close to him and stroked his hair. In a gentle, tearful voice she told him how much she loved him and would miss him. She then said that she would be OK, sad but OK. She talked about their grandkids and the love and support they already had given to her. Then she shared how hard it was to watch him suffer. At that moment, he took a deep breath, and his spirit was freed from his physical body.

There may be rattling sounds in the dying one's chest. These are similar to what you hear in newborns as they take their first breath. As the infant's head emerges from the birth canal, the body naturally creates a force that helps the lungs eliminate the excess fluid in them. The breath slows and weakens in the dying one. The fluid in the lungs remains there. Finally, the force to move the air through the lungs is completely gone, and the dying one takes her last breath.

Almost There

In labor, the stage known as *transition* is the shortest one but also the most difficult. This is the time when the woman's energy is running low, her pain is escalating, and it is hard to help her to relax and remain open to the changes within her body. During the parallel stage in dying, the pain may be difficult to manage. There may be a restlessness present that was not there before, with sounds of moaning. At this time, the caregivers usually need support as well.

In birth, after cervical dilation is complete, the woman experiences a sudden surge of energy. Women describe this stage as a source of direction from within. As the baby's head moves down the birth canal, vaginal tissues begin to stretch as the body prepares for the birth. The baby's head will appear and then sneak back up as if to say, "I am not quite ready." Suddenly the birthing time is here. The baby's head emerges and he takes his first glimpse of his new world.

Miriam:

The memory of the birth of my third son returns as vividly as if it had occurred only moments ago instead of the ten years it has been. The moment I remember is when Patrick's head emerged from the birthing canal. I recall I had just said to everyone in the room, "I'm tired. I think I'll just rest awhile."

Patrick, as if responding to my statement, turned his head up to meet my gaze. Our eyes locked. He very clearly said to me through his eyes, "Hello, Mom. I love you, but now is not the time to rest. Push me home." I did just that. I pushed him out and home to my arms.

There is an energy that is created by birth that is hard to describe. As the woman is pushing, she makes primal noises. She is focused on the outcome now. Each person present either silently pushed with her or cheers loudly. Sometimes it is hard to keep the gentleness of the moment in mind. Too often it sounds like a football game rather than a sacred event. If we hold the woman and her baby in a circle of gentle loving energy, that is the environment the baby will feel as he meets his new world. The dying one, too, is deciding when her time will come. As the death draws nearer, a change can be seen on the face of the dying one. A holy presence blankets her and her loved ones.

One of the nurses we worked with at Hospice House shared her impression of another birth and death parallel:

A man was coming to his last breath. The family and hospice staff gathered around him, each of them breathing along with him. His breaths became slower and more irregular. There were times his breath would stop, and everyone would feel this one would be the last one. He would surely surrender and let go of this body. Yet another breath would be drawn, until finally his face contorted, and he held his breath. He was pushing and pushing. Then there was an extraordinary release as he exhaled one last time, and there was a rush of release and relief from everyone standing at his bedside. It was his last breath; he left his body. At his death moment, he gave everyone such a sense of his spirit being born, a sense that he must now be outside of his body just as a mother who has pushed her last push and released the newborn from her dark canal and womb is now separate from the child's body.

Spiritual Guides

Jan:

I remember a large family who had been keeping a vigil over several days for Jerry, who was a son, father, and husband. His brother came to me and asked why the active phase of dying was taking so long. We talked a long time about how a dying person seems to need reassurance that things will be OK when he is gone. Jim told me that he had told his brother that it was OK that he was dying and that others had as well. "He seems frightened to me," he said. I asked Jim about the people or animals in Jerry's life who he thought would be waiting to guide him as he was dying. Jim spoke of the love Jerry had for his grandma. I watched as he went to Jerry's bedside and told him to follow the light. He spoke about their grandma and all the fun times they had shared. Jim held his hand and moved very close to Jerry. "Look for Grandma, Jerry, she's there for you just as she was when she was here. Maybe she even has some fresh-baked cookies." Jerry seemed to settle down after that. More importantly, Jim led the way for the others to calm Jerry in the same way.

This story offers a good example of the simple ways we can bring comfort and support to the dying one. It is vital that as caregivers we show by example the love and respect that should be given to the dying one. Those people present are acutely aware of our actions. So many times after tending to the dying one with words or actions I will later see the family doing the same thing. We give permission to them to follow what their heart says to do.

Jan:

I recall a young woman dying of cancer. She spoke to me often about her uncle Mike. She spoke of how he made her laugh. "I feel so safe with him, like everything will be OK."

I was working on the night shift so I didn't often get to see Ellen's family. One night Ellen's mom stayed with her. She and I talked about Ellen and the changes that seemed to be happening so rapidly. I shared with her how often Ellen had spoken of the comfort her uncle Mike brought to her. Ellen's mom's eyes grew wide. "Well, that is impossible," she said. "My brother Mike died ten years ago."

We need not be afraid to acknowledge that for many people there is a life after death. If we look to the major religious traditions, we see much written about birth and death and rebirth. *The Tibetan Book of the Dead* sees life as centered around a series of changes that begins with birth and cycles through to death into afterlife and then rebirth.

We have midwived to many people who have had experiences similar to Ellen's. As children many of us have had invisible playmates. Adults often write them off as imaginary. Who is to judge the reality of the guardian angels that accompany us throughout our life? As we are dying, we have the gift of returning to the innocence of our childhood. There were many times that we walked into the rooms of someone who was dying, and although we heard a heartbeat and saw them breathing, we were unable to awaken them. Often, only a short time later, we would find them sitting up, and they would share with us the journey they had just experienced. There were many times we walked into a dying person's room and felt the presence of unseen angels. We have seen the dying one pulling at things in the air that we could not see with our eyes but felt with our hearts. To be present with those birthing or dying, we need to acknowledge that we cannot apply our usual earthly rules and regulations. They are experiences that are not governed by our way of seeing things, but by the wings of angels.

Often, it is the midwife's role to help communicate to the baby or the dying one that it is time to be born or to die. The baby and the dying one both choose their moment of transition, but often they must feel welcomed, loved, and encouraged.

Jan:

I was present at a birth that made me aware of the importance of the baby also needing to be encouraged to join this earth family. The labor had been difficult and the baby was not breathing following the delivery. I could hear his heartbeat, so I knew there was life present. It was as if his spirit was unable to connect with his physical body. We continued to resuscitate the baby. I suddenly thought about how vital it was for the dying one to be told that it was OK to leave. It was clear that sometimes the newborn needs to be told it's OK to join us here. I called the baby's dad over. "Talk to him," I said. "Let him know it is

OK to be here and that this is his new home." The dad said, "Hey, slugger, remember me? I am the guy you kicked all the time. Your mom and I have waited a long time to meet you." The baby slowly began to breathe, and I encouraged his dad to keep talking to him. The baby suddenly pinked up and let out a loud screech that told us he had indeed joined us here on earth.

In a similar birth, it was the aunt who brought baby Derek fully into his body. She yelled very loudly at him, "OK, Derek James, this is your auntie talking. You need to start breathing, young man." He immediately followed directions and let out a lusty cry.

From Darkness into the Light

We live in a time when many accounts are being written about near-death experiences. Although that is not the topic of this book, it offers a way to validate in some way the things we see in our work with the dying. Anya Foos-Graber, author of *Deathing*, writes, "Death can't be ignored for long; it won't stay quietly out of sight, democratic as it is."

Near-death experiences give us insight into the process of death and dying. They can be compared to the state of mind people attain during meditation. Stephen Levine, author of *Who Dies?* describes the process of dying perfectly. "You are with the one who is dying in the same way you are with yourself. Open, honest, and caring. . . . If it hurts, it hurts. If it makes you happy, it makes you happy. . . . Just hear the truth that the moment has to offer."

People who have near-death experiences share similar stories. In many accounts, they see people who come to meet them and assist them on their journey. Many describe a tunnel with a bright light at the end toward which they traveled. A feeling of utter and complete peace encompasses them.

Just as birth is a process, so is dying. During the pre-active phase of dying, people will often flit in and out of their bodies. It is as if they are exploring where they are going and becoming comfortable with it. It is their sharing of these out-of-body experiences that assists us in knowing what support is needed during the active phase of dying.

Miriam:

I was speaking to the wife of a dying man one evening. The woman had spent many hours at the bedside of her husband, who was actively dying. She told me, "It's amazing. Sometimes I get the sensation that he has left his body. His color changes; I can barely detect him breathing or feel his heart. Then all of a sudden, it's as if he reenters his body. His color is pinker, he's noticeably breathing, and I can feel his heart. I wish he could talk to me and tell me what happens during those times."

I spent time with her explaining that others have had the very same experience. It's as if a person's spirit experiments with leaving the body. This particular man spent many hours apparently coming and going. I remember how faithfully his wife would stay with him. She would tell him to take as much time as he needed and reassured him that he would not be alone throughout this vigil. It was a long, arduous labor for him to leave his body that final time, but she kept her promise and remained with him until the very end.

Beyond Words

Birth and death elicit strong responses from all who are present. For many, words cannot explain the spiritual nature of what has been witnessed. Following a birth or death, there is a strong need to retell the experience. It is a way of making it real, of creating some order for the experience. The process of retelling how birth or death looked, felt, and sounded is important. It is an event that influences us for a lifetime. Memories of this experience will drift in and out of our conscious thought for the rest of our lives. They help us come to terms with our own existence and eventual death.

The following memory speaks to the importance of talking about the dying process. It is a process that offers something unique for all who take part. The layers of grief are interwoven into a quilt of stories by all who share a loss through death. We begin our healing by talking about it.

Miriam:

Colleen's process of dying was marked by her overwhelming fear. She was horrified at the way her cervical cancer had ravaged her body and was anxious about her pain. Her left leg was grossly swollen from her hip to her toes'; this was how the cancer had spread, affecting her lymphatic system as well as her blood circulation. In addition to her physical distress, she was concerned that her caregivers would abandon her.

Each time I cared for Colleen, I was faced with the challenge of responding to this enormous pain and fear. Together, Colleen and I would explore ways to allow her feelings to be present and then replace them with a sense of painlessness and calmness. We made a great deal of progress with medication as well, but Colleen also responded wonderfully to simple listening and quiet suggestion. Often by the end of my shift, she would be resting peacefully with a beautiful smile on her laughing Irish face. We worked through a great deal of pain and fear, Colleen and I.

I needed to see Colleen's body when she died. She would never let me speak to her about what happened to people when they died; it was as if it caused her pain just to think about it. After her death, her body was prepared to be received by the funeral home. I arrived at her room before the funeral representatives had arrived. She lay dressed in the sweatshirt, jeans, and Reeboks that she had carefully selected shortly after admission to Hospice House. The people she had loved most in her life were gathered around her bed. They gave me time to hug Colleen and say good-bye.

Colleen's mother was the first to share the experience of her daughter's death. As she spoke, her friends would add to the description. The memory was clearly vivid for each of them. They told of her every struggle and what they did to comfort her. Astronomical amounts of morphine and Inapsine had been given intravenously. Her mother exclaimed, "It was as if the medicine would help for a short while, and then she would get upset and try to get out of bed. Each time she tried to move, she would feel the pain again." Her friend would explain how they would take turns holding her hand and comforting her, constantly talking to her, letting her know she wasn't alone. "That seemed to help. She would almost relax and then sit up again. Finally it was somewhere in the middle of the night that she was able to relax and just have small periods of time when she would be restless. At one point, she no longer tried to move. She became more and more peaceful. We stayed with her through it all. It seemed the nurses were in here just when she needed something. It was a long night and an exhausting one for everyone, but she finally died peacefully."

As the conversation continued, it moved on to memories of Colleen's life that brought joy and laughter. It was important for me to hear about her passage. I had been concerned that her dying might be difficult. Her family and friends had let me know that Colleen had not suffered alone and without consolation. Their steadfast vigil was an answer to my prayer for Colleen.

It seems that if I witness a birth or death, the need to retell that powerful experience is of paramount importance. I will treasure those memories her family so graciously shared. I will also hold the memory of Colleen's soft, laughing Irish eyes in my heart.

Too often we have seen people move much too quickly following a birth or a death. It is critical for us to move slowly following these sacred events. Whether a spirit has entered the world or left it, we must create a holy space for the transition to occur.

Rites of Passage

We do not regard birth and death as separate experiences. They exist within each other. This rhythm of life will not be deterred. It may ebb and flow, but life will continue its course of constant change. Just as a baby grows to maturity within the mother's womb and must leave, so will the body mature to its end and once again leave its place of shelter.

The finality of birth and death changes all who are connected with the process. Death is recognized as the final breath is drawn. The room becomes quiet as everyone begins to realize fully that a miracle has occurred. The tears begin to flow. What you hold in your heart is the memory of a new life.

4

Midwives and the Labor of Dying

Of all the similarities between the paths of birth and death, perhaps the most important and striking is that both birth and death involve a physical labor. During these labors, our bodies and souls are pushed to their limits and beyond. In the midst of the struggles of labor, either in birth or death, it is often only the midwife's voice that breaks through and comforts or strengthens. More than any other factor of the dying process, it is being there during this labor that should concern the midwife most. Because of this, the labor of dying merits its own discussion here.

Having worked in both obstetrics and hospice, Jan's experiences in these two fields have provided many of the stories in this book. It may be somewhat surprising to find out, however, that she once served at a birth and a death on the very same day. Her description of that day provides some lessons here.

Jan:

I recall a weekend I was working when I had two patients in active labor. One was experiencing the labor of birth, the other the labor of dying. As I mid-wived to them, the care I offered to each of them was similar. The questions I was asked by both were similar. "When will this labor end? Is everything happening as it should? When should we call our families?" The emotional responses were also similar. "I feel like I can't keep going. I am so tired." Both had the need to go inside and be still. The physical complaints were remarkably similar. The nausea and vomiting increased as the contractions increased. The headaches from the fatigue and the body aches are overwhelming.

My care centered around providing comfort and support to the laboring ones and their families. As the labors progressed, both needed medications to ease the discomfort. Hot compresses aided in their relaxation. Sitting quietly by as they labored brought comfort to their weary hearts. I offered therapeutic touch to bring them some tranquillity and alleviate some of the physical symptoms of these natural processes. I made assessments of their progress. Most important of all, I remembered often that this was the patients' process, not mine. Through the darkness and the pain, there was empowerment of who they were and what they were capable of.

Our role as midwives is to teach people how to function independently of us, to be there for support and guidance, but to teach them to trust their bodies and their instincts about what they or their loved one needs.

In preparing for childbirth, it is also part of the role of midwives and childbirth educators to explain the labor process as a series of understandable stages, to make the entire journey seem less strange and frightening. There is a deep significance for both a woman and her partner in knowing that they will follow all the known stages of the birthing process just as thousands of generations of their ancestors have also done—and yet, they will do so in just their own way.

So it is with the dying. It is valuable for the dying and their caregivers to know the stages through which they shall pass so that the experience is not simply fright and pain, but is given order and sacredness. Just as the dying person's female ancestors went through stages of childbirth, so have all his ancestors also gone through the stages of dying.

We begin this chapter with a discussion of the physical stages of labor in childbirth and how they correspond to the stages of labor in death. But we don't want to dwell on these too long. We don't wish to give the impression that being a midwife to the dying involves technical training or knowledge; it is much more important to follow your instincts and be yourself. We will take the opportunity to focus on what the caregiver brings to the labor process, what he or she can do in special situations and in particular areas. The chapter closes with a series of charts that the dying and caregivers can use to follow the stages of dying and give comfort and ease during this time.

The Labor of Birth

Through the ages, midwives have had a basic understanding of the process of labor and delivery in childbirth. The labor is divided into three stages. The first begins with the onset of regular contractions—the tightening, rhythmic motions of the uterus—and ends with the complete dilation of the cervix. Generally the process takes eight to fourteen hours. Just as in the labor of dying, the process is unique to each individual. This first stage helps prepare the woman's body to release the infant within. The infant and mother both experience physical and emotional changes that help motivate the birth to occur.

The transition phase occurs when the patient is in active labor, after the first stage. By this time, the uterine contractions last forty-five to sixty seconds and occur every one to two minutes. Exhausted and wondering if there is an end to this, the woman usually feels as if she has just hiked up an impossibly tall mountain. Although transition is the shortest phase of labor, it is often the most difficult. Emotional intensity is heightened. A women needs to be prepared for this and encouraged to think of it as a normal part of the process.

The second stage of labor is the actual release of the infant from the womb. The cervix is now fully dilated, and contractions are one to two minutes apart, lasting fifty to ninety seconds. The mother will have a profound urge to push at this time. This stage gives full meaning to the term *labor*. The woman will work harder here than at any other time in her life. The second stage may last only a few minutes or two to three hours. It is essential for both the mother and the midwife to connect spiritually to the baby during this stage. Just as in death, it is important to tell the baby to "follow the light."

The third stage of labor is the delivery of the placenta. The placenta separates from the wall of the uterus and releases from the womb. This process can take from five to 30 minutes. The labor and delivery are now complete.

The Labor of Dying

If you desire to understand death, look to the body. Sudden death within minutes means a critical function has collapsed, with either the heart or the lungs ceasing to work. Life ends abruptly. The "labor" is short. The shock of death is intensely perceived. It is quite profound. A great deal of time and effort by others is required to sort through what that loss means. The letting go of that person must be done without his or her physical presence.

There is another kind of dying, however. It is slower yet still distinct in its process. This dying could take hours, days, or weeks. The following pages describe in detail the labor of this dying process. Although it differs from sudden death, the experience is certainly as profound. It does, however, afford the healing element of time.

We have identified three stages in the labor of dying that correspond to the stages in childbirth. These are Stage I: preactive labor, the "beginning" of physical death; Stage II: active labor, the transition phase of dying; and Stage III: death. We are often asked whether there are major differences in the way these stages play out, depending on the illness. In fact, as long as a labor is not extremely compressed, the process for someone with cancer, another with AIDS, and a third with pneumonia is roughly the same, although additional symptoms may present themselves depending on the illness. In the end, we feel that individuals' unique qualities have more to do with the differences between labors than the diseases themselves.

Preactive labor, the first stage, may last from days to weeks. Its physical changes are very similar to those of birth. The person will eat and drink less, and her breathing patterns will change. There may be an increase in pain, confusion, and/or weakness. Body temperature very often fluctuates, and sleeping cycles are disrupted. There may be a noted sensitivity to sight, sound, smell, and activity.

The accompanying emotional/spiritual changes can be noted by the dying one's withdrawal from all but a chosen few. Some may cry more frequently and fear being alone (especially at night). There may be an increase in restlessness, agitation, and anxiety. Anger, impatience, and depression may be more pronounced. Others find a strong need to discuss their approaching death or to remember those who have died. Many desire to "finish business" by stating or restating their desire to have no extraordinary measures taken to prolong their lives. Their wills may be completed. The funeral arrangements and a discussion or arrangement of their memorials might be their final concern. Loved ones may be gathered to say the final good-byes. Simply put, these actions are taken to create closure to their lives.

The second stage in dying is the active labor. This may last hours to days. As in birth, the intensity of the process is dramatically escalated. The physical changes are quite pronounced. The skin may begin cooling and mottling, starting with the toes and fingers and working toward the center of the body. Temperature fluctuations may continue, including high fevers or the chills. The skin color becomes dusky or gray, sometimes translucent. There may be increased lung congestion, and breathing will be increasingly irregular for most. The ability to communicate verbally generally diminishes. Most people will have lost the ability to swallow more than a sip at this stage. Some will tolerate only the sponging of the mouth. The ability to get out of bed, even to a bedside commode is generally gone. There is a general deterioration of the body (including unpleasant odors and loss of bladder and bowel control). Remember, dying is a process, and during the stages of dying, you are adapting to many changes.

The emotional/spiritual changes in active labor encompass different qualities from the preactive. Some may have an experience similar to the transitional phase of birthing. This may include an increase in restlessness, agitation, and anxiety. Some may continue to experience fear. Others may simply relax into the changes his or her body is experiencing. There may be a calmness, an acceptance, or an intensified awareness of his or her spiritual source. Loved ones who gather may see signs of relaxation when the dying one hears their voices or feels their touch.

The final and third stage of dying is the actual moment of death. This means that the heart and lungs have ceased to function. It may take minutes to complete. Just prior to this, the dying one may exhibit a need to push as if birthing. Their breathing may gradually stop. The skin color dramatically changes to a gray. An involuntary loss of stool or urine may occur. The mouth and eyes may remain open. Although this stage lasts only a few moments, its impact lasts a lifetime.

The Importance of Midwives

The beginnings of the art of midwifery are lost in the mists of the very beginnings of humanity. The first recorded account of midwifery is found in the very first book of the Bible: "And it came to pass when she was in hard labor, that the midwife said unto her, fear not . . ." (Gen. 35:16–18).

Today, the formal understanding of the word *midwife* has evolved substantially to include men and women with special training and experience. It is likely, however, that our ancient forebears would not have looked at the task of assisting in childbirth and assisting in dying as requiring special knowledge. In the days before modern medical technology, birth and death were looked at as natural parts of the life cycle, which encompassed crop cycles, the raising and hunting of animals, and preparation for the changing seasons. We can picture how the births and deaths of our ancestors were understood from what we know of native cultures. As a need for help presented itself, men and women drew together as a community to give it. All shared in the care of those who were dying and birthing.

Today, we are trying to reclaim this connection between midwifery, community, and family as we look beyond traditional medical structures as the sole providers of support during times of life-challenging illness. In both birth and death, midwives are assuming their importance once again.

As you begin the journey of the midwife, we encourage you to look deep within yourself for the courage and wisdom of your ancestors: they have done this work, and they have passed on their secrets deep within your heart. Always remember to preserve the sacredness of the experiences of birth and death. Remember that each is the opening and closing of the same circle.

The following is a poem that Anne Pitkin wrote following her husband's death. We graciously bow to her wisdom.

THE MIDWIVES

Just within the limits
of the visible, this dusk
is bright, spacious,
the weather kind, as if
mercy were, after all,
the current bearing our flimsy vessels
into shore, or out.

The room is darkened
where the family waits
with him. His soul, attached
to its malaise,
tumbles, tumbles
in its ocean,
inaccessible.

Across the street
the gray stones of the church
dapple with the sunlight.
Two gulls settle, each
on one arm of the small cross,
white against the sky stirring
in its nest of new leaves.
A third hovers, crying.

One by one, the nurses
come to help him.

THE TRUE WORK OF DYING

They know the infant
rocking like a sailboat
in its warm, amniotic sea
does not want to be born, clings
to its host. Its host.

The body, suffers. It may be,
the family speculates
from time to time, that breath
is not the only utterance, may be
the only song is but a bone lodged
in the singer's throat, no more
beyond the visible
than that.

The room is quiet,
This is it, the wife keeps saying
to the room, dim and quiet
where the end twists, unheard,
to its conclusion.
Finishing her shift, Sarah checks in,
whispers, Pulse steady
but the kidneys aren't working. Easy now.
Maybe he knows.
Maybe he is the weather, his breath
growing less and less relevant
to the body, to the family
that waits, transfixed
by this occasion.

One by one, the nurses tend him.
Familiar with the universe,
its howl, its silence, they hold
wife, daughters, small son,

hold them to the truth,
invisible, of mercy. The world
swings on its bright
and fragile chain, swings.

To the breath of one lung,
quiet as the pool of sunlight
traveling certainly
and imperceptibly across the floor
at home, across a yellow leaf
from the begonia plant,
or a curl of dust,
one tennis shoe.

No shadows here.
No sunlight, nothing
but the family, and history
calling its one name,
the world retreating, smaller,
brighter, deeper into the cold
blue radiance of what is lost.
Too soon, the small son says.
Once he said, musing
on this day, the father once said,

It can never be too soon.
Now the body suffers
but he doesn't know. Maybe
he returns to the cradle
where life shudders,
makes its leap, and blossoms

or fails, or blooms,
then fails, where the infant, racked

with possibility, still clings,
clings to its host
the failing body, burst bud, blossom
loosening its grip. She calls
Mark, the night nurse, says,
But no, not yet, says Children!

Mark checks the pulse, waits, then
says quietly, as if
a pigeon has been turned loose
with a message on its legs, says,
I think he's going. Yes,
he's leaving us. He's leaving us.
Gently now . . .

—ANNE PITKIN

In her book *Deathing,* Anya Foos-Graber writes, "Midwiving at death opens a way to free up dying people so they can utilize the highest potential of the transition called death and experience it as a peak moment, a culmination of life."

Serving as a midwife brings with it great responsibilities. Your heart is opened not just by the joy you experience, but also by the pain. You make a commitment to be present with the dying one through it all, not just for a brief moment.

The professional hospice worker, in particular, may be called away from home in the middle of the night. She becomes attached to a beeper that creates a lifeline between her and her patients. Her own family often wonders if she will be home for dinner.

But most importantly, the midwife is often the privileged one who will witness the patient have his or her first or last bath, take his or her first or last breath. She will stand in awe of the moment-to-moment changes in the faces of those experiencing birth and death. She holds the patient in her arms for the first or the last time. It is the midwife—you—who, when the experience is complete, will walk away a new person, whose heart has been opened to yet a deeper level of feeling and understanding. Through the experience, you are given life.

Of course, being a midwife may mean different things depending on what special role one is called to fill. Take the example of Jan's family who midwived to Grandpa Joe as he lay dying. Aunt Dolores was at his head whispering encouragement; the grandchildren would each come in their own time and their own way to say their good-byes. Shirley was in charge of providing care and comfort for the children. Susan was at home arranging for meals to be brought to the nursing home. Uncle Van would come in once an hour to check on Grandpa's feet and report on any changes in their color or temperature. A dear friend kept others aware by telephone of any changes. Every one of these people served as midwives to Grandpa as he journeyed toward death. No job was any less important than any other. They were a community honoring the dying one. The following song was written by singer/songwriter Marie Eaton. It speaks to the pain that is experienced with change and the healing element of time.

TAKE YOUR TIME
... I stood outside the door
my life fell in pieces
the pattern was broken
I asked my heart
how will I make it
the tears they will drown me
will I ever laugh again? Ah but

95

Take your time
it takes time
Time will take you and teach you how
if you take your time.

Caring for the Caregiver

Just as it is important to attend to the changes in the dying one as her labor progresses, it is equally important to pay attention to changes in the caregiver. The time of dying is profoundly stressful for everyone concerned. Care during labor is required on a twenty-four-hour basis, and few people in a home environment can keep up this pace for long without assistance. However, if the caregiver for the dying one is not able to withstand the physical, emotional, and spiritual demands at this time—even with the support of all available resources—they need not try to continue on as the primary caregiver.

In our hospice work, we find that the majority of caregivers at home *are* able to respond to the increased stress and demands of active labor. It is possible because there are so many comfort and support measures available for them. We have provided charts at the end of this chapter to help align the caregiver's response during each stage of the dying labor with that of the dying one. Suggestions for support that we have found to be most helpful are included.

During preactive labor, it is not uncommon for caregivers also to experience physical changes such as fatigue or insomnia, stomach upset, fearfulness, and headache. These occur because the time demands and intensity of care increase dramatically. The midwife may need to assist with bathing, oral care, middle-of-the-night sleeplessness or restlessness, or increased frequency of medications. The reality of the dying one's dramatic decline invariably brings on the awareness that death is much closer. This triggers emotional responses, which can manifest themselves in guilt, anger, depression, relief, despair, and/or withdrawal for those providing care.

How each of us will cope depends on a multitude of factors, ranging from the quality of existing resources and support, the ability to seek assistance, the availability of resources, and the interpersonal responses of all those involved in the decision-making process. If the caregiving depends only on one person, the ability to provide competent care will probably be compromised. Finding people who will be of help is paramount.

When demands on the caregiver increase, it is important for him or her to take inventory of his or her feelings and strength. The support measures we have suggested in our charts focus on methods to alleviate stress and tension (e.g., taking hot baths, walking, exercise, sleep, regular meals, prayer, meditation, and quiet reflection). This combined with having others close by to listen, give hugs, and provide assistance with care will be invaluable to creating a peaceful atmosphere. We list these measures as a beginning, a reminder of how important the need to care for oneself during this time is.

In our experience, the quality of care provided for the dying one increases significantly when caregivers take care of themselves first. The measures described do not take a great deal of time. It is amazing what a ten- to twenty-minute break will provide. Hospice volunteer programs around the country have been a great asset to families in this regard. Trained volunteers in these programs are usually available for up to four hours one day a week (check with your local hospice for details). Scheduling time is not as difficult as it may seem, especially as family and friends gather during the labor of dying. So many of the memories we include speak to how each person invited to this event is able to receive and lend others support. It is usually the small gifts that provide the greatest relief. Meals provided by friends, an hour or two respite from the bedside of the dying one, a gift of music, flowers, or a card. The ways to share during this time are countless.

Caregivers who are unable to provide sufficient care at this point should not regard this as a failure or short-coming; it only means a different care scenario is required. A great deal of the work of a hospice team during the labor phase is to recognize any need for increased support or other options for a beleaguered caregiver, including the transfer of the patient to a facility such as a nursing home, hospice unit, or hospital. There are *always* options. It is often possible to access family, friends, churches, or community resources to find additional care-givers. In addition, trained professionals can be hired as in-home caregivers.

Of course, the labor will eventually progress to Stage II—active labor. Physical, emotional, and spiritual changes will peak in intensity at this time. There will be little doubt death is imminent. The caregiver may also continue to exhibit signs and symptoms of stress. They may have diarrhea, backache, fatigue and/or insomnia, loss of appetite, and tears. The emotional or spiritual responses could contain sorrow, fear, loss, abandonment, separation, guilt from wanting the death to come, numbness, tenderness, closeness to those present, an intensified sense of spiritual strength, and/or a sense of peace or well-being.

During this challenging period, it is important to remember an intensity will exist far beyond most past experiences. As we have discussed previously, it is helpful to remember the intensity of childbirth to give perspective to this time. Some may equate the death experience with the most joyful, sorrowful, and glorious times in their lives. One way these memories can be helpful is to examine the outcome with a positive reflection. The memories we have included in this book so often speak to the transformation of people during this time of loss. It seems lives can be enriched in miraculous and unexpected ways during the labor of a loved one's death. We continually are told by caregivers who have completed this experience that they would go through it in the same way again if given the choice no matter how exhausted, frustrated, angry, or sorrowful for them the time had been.

Talking to the dying one is of great value in your spiritual work. Some may feel moved to speak of beloved people or pets who have died. Others give permission for the dying one to let go. Some pray aloud or in silence. Touching is also a marvelous support, not only for the dying one, but for the caregiver. It is a physical way to say good-bye, and this becomes the time for the final good-byes. Trust what your heart directs you to do. Continue to take care of yourself. Perhaps, most importantly, take your time. Even though time may be limited to hours or days, move slowly and quietly. It is in the silence that God speaks loudest to us.

The moment of death is the final stage. It is not until the death moment that you will realize your response in totality. Allow yourself enough time to respond in your own special way. An initial period of time is inevitably necessary to understand that the death has occurred. This might take several minutes for some. The moments after death are a time for saying good-bye, paying tribute to the loved one's life through the spoken word, and honoring the body by keeping it covered, gentle cleansing, changing garments, or staying with the body until funeral home representatives arrive. This is also a time for the caregiver to pray, honor his or her needs for rest or time alone, and allow feelings to surface. See our discussion in Chapter 7 for additional insights into ways to honor this most sacred event.

Personalized Caring

Midwives offer something very special during labor; they value its process and respect its integrity. They can serve the whole person and not just the body. Not enough value is placed on the importance of those comfort measures that don't require a physician's order. To sit quietly in someone's company and listen to the words they speak demand great strength. Quiet touch through gentle massage, reassuring pats, and comforting hugs all provide healing to a weary heart and body. The term *love medicine,* taken from the title of a recent novel, seems to apply here.

Family members will often say they are not sure what to do for the dying one. Do not be afraid to ask the person, What do you need right now? Trust your inner voice to guide you.

We have found music to be a powerful healer when words are unable to reach the pain and loss of the dying experience. Songs often give voice to your feelings that you cannot express. The melody and rhythm can illuminate and release feelings blocked or held within. Music can also bring light and laughter to a sad heart. Although dying is filled with loss, it can also be filled with joy.

Take time to recall what kind of music provided comfort to your loved one. An important question to ask yourself at all times is, Am I providing comfort to the dying one or myself? Am I doing this to take away my discomfort or my loved one's discomfort? Often we mistakenly choose music that relaxes the caregiver but not the dying one.

Give yourself permission to release your laughter. The journey of dying intensifies emotions. Holding in tears or laughter is not necessary. This is a time for letting go. It is a time of honesty. It is a precious time that is limited. Give yourself permission to experience your emotions honestly and openly. Expressing feelings is part of the healing process—for you as well as the dying one. Later in this chapter, we will tell a story about the healing laughter can bring.

Remember, there may be days when nothing you do feels right or helpful. A person's body changes rapidly at the time of death. The process is not comfortable, and the need for care increases dramatically. It is not a time to remain alone or to take the entire responsibility on your shoulders. The chart on pages 102 and 103 will provide some ideas for care during this critical time. Let your inner voice guide you with your choices.

Toward a Peaceful Death

The Dying experience is one filled with many emotions. The intensity of these emotions will vary from moment to moment. As hospice nurses, we have tried to identify the ways that caregivers can assist the dying in their attempts to transcend this intensity. The experience of a state of well-being—even during a time of crisis—is a worthwhile goal. We desire to make a truly peaceful

THE TRUE WORK OF DYING

PERSONALIZED CARE

Quiet listening

Sit quietly, perhaps touching gently. Be honest about your own feelings of sadness or loss.

Massage

Always honor the dying one's boundaries and be guided by them. Some massage therapists are trained to work with dying people; you can learn from them but know that your gentle touch can be healing, too. Use oils or lotions that will not irritate the skin. You may want to play quiet music to aid in relaxation.

Therapeutic touch

This is done by a person trained in the art of therapeutic touch. The method words with a person's energy field to bring comfort and relief from physical and emotional pain.

Sound

The sounds a dying one hears are important. Sound also affects those who are caring for this person. Avoid disruptive or disturbing noises, such as television in the background. Choose music that brings comfort. Be creative with your choices. Consider contacting The Chalice of Repose, based in Missoula, Mont. This organization provides harp music designed to assist the dying in relaxing and letting go.

Family gatherings

Create a gathering of the dying one's choice of people (i.e., a special dinner, singing together, playing games). Honor his or her fatigue level. Remember to include the children; they can bring a smile when no one else can. If a large group is too tiring for the person, create a video or audiotape with messages. Make time for each person to be alone with the dying one. Be honest with each other about the sadness of letting go.

A picture board

Have family and friends gather pictures of times

shared together. Place them on a bulletin board near the bed, where everyone can see them. As the death draws nearer, the board will provide comfort to everyone.

Books

Many people enjoy being read to. Books that speak to their spiritual beliefs bring comfort and can help alleviate fear. Many books are available on audiotape when your voice gives out! Hearing is still very acute even though it seems the dying one cannot hear you. We know the difference a loved one's voice makes in the dying one's comfort level. This is still an integral part of the support you give to him or her.

Room environment

Pay close attention to the atmosphere created by the room environment. A comfortable bed, medical equipment and supplies should be easily accessible, as well as personal belongings important to the dying one, such as a familiar blanket or pillow, which will promote comfort. Caregivers should have the ability to change the room temperature, open or close windows, brighten or dim the lights, and adjust the environment to comfort.

Loved ones

Honor the dying one's desire to see other people. This is the time to invite those who bring prayer, rituals, relaxation, visualization, and/or guided imageries if desired by the dying one. As always be sure to have permission from the dying one or his or her family. Continue to honor what you believe the person would want at this time even though he or she may be unable to tell you verbally!

Atmosphere

Move slowly, quietly, and gently. Keep extra stimulus to a minimum.

death possible for every person. We now address a person's emotional and physical needs and how we can help the dying to let go and achieve rest.

Being Honest

There is a certain kind of honesty between two people or within your soul that is possible when we consciously choose to live in each moment, despite whatever it holds and whatever we feel about it. Those who can offer this honest presence to the dying offer a priceless resource: true relationship. The dying often fear being physically alone. The greatest gift we can give the dying is to share precious moments with hearts and minds wide open.

Miriam:
Whenever I think of honesty, I think of Ted, a young man whom I cared for at Hospice House. Ted had an amazing amount of energy and caring, considering that he was entering the last stages of AIDS. For instance, he religiously kept to a ritual of saying good night to all the hospice patients before he turned in each night. Going from room to room, he would spend time with each person talking about their day or at least offer a quick wave and a smile.

Often I had spoken to Ted about places he would like to visit. Just before Thanksgiving, I invited him for an outing to a historic house, the Pittock Mansion, which is decorated each Christmas. Upon arrival, we were informed that the opening for Christmas viewing wouldn't be for another week. I can remember almost blurting out, "But he's dying! He may not have another week!" I held back my words, fearing they might be offensive to him.

Instead we went to a gallery where Ted had worked prior to his illness. The exhibit was a series of rooms with the grayest, most depressing images of cities devastated by bombing in World War II. People's faces in the photographs were distraught, their bodies devastated by lack of food. I could not believe we were spending Ted's precious time looking at these portraits of darkness.

I heard Ted call to me from the last room. "Miriam, come here quick . . . This is beautiful." I walked in to see him intently gazing at a glorious picture. It was the image of a gate of a city of destruction, opening into an incredible burst of color—an English garden, sun drenched and filled with light and life. Ted said, "That's where I'm going. Isn't it beautiful? I get to go there." We stayed for a while longer jut gazing at the wonder of this image.

When I dropped him off, Ted and I made a date to go to the Pittock Mansion the next week. But three or four days later, he began to run a high temperature. His condition deteriorated rapidly. I realized he wouldn't be able to make our date. I came to the hospice on the day of our appointment, not to work, but to pick up some items for a project.

Ted's mother came to the office I was in and said, "I am so glad you stopped in. Ted has been calling your name for hours. He insists he must get ready to go out. Would you please stop in to see him?"

I was stunned as I walked into his room. His body was so close to dying. I leaned down and spoke gently into his ear to let him know I was there. He said, "I don't think I can make it today. I'm sorry." I said,

"Oh, Ted, it's all right. I know you need to go to that beautiful garden we saw. I can't come with you yet, but I'll be there soon. Good-bye, my friend. I will miss you." He died later that evening.

Honesty is for me a willingness to be in the moment. Ted and I shared the honesty our moments had for us. It's the only way I know how to be honest with myself and with others in a meaningful way. Each person deserves this gift, especially during our times of greatest trial.

Providing an Environment of Comfort and Respect

In hospice care at home, the creation of the dying space is important. It should be clear that the person who is dying holds the attention of others: the dying are completely vulnerable and in need of total care at this time. Should the caregivers themselves be unable to provide the care, it is vital that a place be found that accommodates the dying one.

Miriam was privileged to work with a family who had a marvelous ability to savor each day taking care of their mother. Their story points to many of the considerations in providing a satisfactory dying space.

Miriam:

I once worked with a remarkable woman dying from metastisized cancer who created her own dying space in her bedroom, which had a large window overlooking a garden. The hospital bed was dressed with an enormous down comforter atop flannel sheets. Her bedside table held fresh flowers, an assortment of food and drink, and her favorite books, letters, and pictures. The bedside commode was placed strategically to accommodate her needs. An oxygen machine was neatly tucked into a corner with the tubing placed carefully to provide quick access. Her medication and supplies were neatly organized and placed for optimal use. Comfortable chairs for family and friends were available but limited to two. (This kept the number of people in her room down.) A tape player close by was continually fed with her favorite music. There was a small heater to be turned on during bathing to keep her warm. It was delightful to spend time in this space. I enjoyed it each time the decor would change for the current celebration or holiday. This space truly reflected the presence of this marvelous woman.

She began to let us know that her time of dying was approaching. She had long since resolved her issues with each of her children. She celebrated Thanksgiving, birthdays, Christmas, and New Year's in her last few months. The final celebration would be the marriage of one of her daughters. After so many months of celebrations, she began to speak to each person who held a special place in her heart and life. She created her dying space by saying good-bye to each and every one. Once the good-byes were completed, the three children who would remain began their vigil.

During one visit, she asked me to read out of the early version of this book. I read to her the chapter on birth and death parallels. By this time, her body was clearly in the active phase of dying. Each time that I read about a change that could occur during the dying process she would say, "Yes, that's right. That's what is happening to me right now." I read until finally she said, "Oh, that has not happened yet." We spoke about the changes to come. She asked me to describe how the breathing changes, how we would keep her comfortable. "I am at peace, but this is taking longer than I expected."

My final visit came. I had already said good-bye to her and she to me. With barely energy left to breathe, she said, "I just can't let go. I'm stuck. How do I get there?" Her children had joined us in the room. We all gave her encouragement. I'm not sure of the exact words we said except I know they were the words she needed to hear at that moment. She drifted off into a deeper place within herself. Finally, she let go of her concern that she wasn't doing something "just right." Her face was relaxed and peaceful when I left.

In general, the room dedicated to the dying one's care should contain the necessary medical equipment to provide comfort and support along with the symbols and images important to the dying one, caregivers, family, and friends. Each person entering the room should easily recognize and acknowledge the sacred role of the space.

The challenge to meet the needs of others can be profound. Where the family in the previous story came together seamlessly to offer support, other families may find it harder to coordinate or agree upon care measures. In such cases, it is important for someone—hopefully a team of hospice professionals—to oversee the process of labor.

Miriam recently worked with one such family who presented a complex scenario.

MIDWIVES AND THE LABOR OF DYING

Miriam:

The patient was a young mother in the final stages of brain cancer with two sons, aged three and eight. The challenges began from the time the physician's referral was made to our hospice team. There were not only three physicians involved in directing her care, but at least a dozen or so family and friends providing the hands-on care at her home.

The woman and her husband were faced with making decisions in a relatively short period of time. This woman desired to remain at home, but this choice was not necessarily a goal for those close to her. In fact, it seemed each person connected with this family had their own idea of how care should be delivered and what was the best course of action. Her husband's family took turns weekly in caring for her and the children. Her mother would spend time taking her out of the home for socializing. Their church community provided numerous people to clean the house weekly and provide daily meals. Hired caregivers in conjunction with volunteer nurses from the church cared for her on a twenty-four-hour-a-day basis. The family used the hospice team to be the one entity that received input from everyone else—family, friends, church, home health care agencies, and physicians.

The goal was to provide gentle, loving care, competently delivered. Our hospice team was able to support this family by listening to their directions and using each resource in a manner appropriate to the woman's needs. The challenge for our team to respond to was intense due to the layers of complex relationships between the family members. Our team responded with compassion, perseverance, and patience. Gradually a rhythm of care was realized using the best of each person who came to help.

When an infant is not nurtured with touch and caring, he does not thrive. When a dying person is not cared for in the same way, she cannot achieve all the healing possible through the process of dying.

Many caregivers shy away from touching the dying one because they don't know what will feel good; or they may be afraid of hurting the dying one. We tell them to follow their hearts. Ask this question: what felt good before the person was sick? How did she like to be touched and comforted? Sometimes her disease may cause her pain when she is touched. You may need to redefine the ways you can bring physical comfort. A cool washcloth to the forehead or gentle hand holding can bring comfort in the midst of pain.

The story of the little girl Alexandra (whom we introduced in Chapter 2) and her need for touch is relevant here.

Jan:

Alex's breathing had become labored; speaking was difficult. Any activity requiring much physical energy was not possible. Yet even at this time, she reached out to her family.

Alex lay in her mom and dad's bed with three loving generations gathered around her; Great Great-grandma Dappie, Great-grammie Billie, Great-Great gramp, Great-grandpa Ed, Papa Ron, Nona Renee, her mom and dad and brother Zachary. One by one, she gave each a task. Using the peppermint lotion that she liked, someone massaged her feet, another massaged her hands, still another her legs. When they stopped, she would wiggle her feet for more.

In the midst of their sorrow, she helped them to find a quiet place. In the midst of their fear, she helped them remember this was still their little Alex—only her body had changed, not her spirit.

One of the difficult things about supporting someone through the dying process is that we must redefine who we are and what our dreams are for the one who is dying. Physical touch in whatever way it is given must be given carefully. Always remember to confirm in your heart that any measure is a love-filled measure. Above all else, take your time.

The monk Thomas Merton once observed that there is "laughter at the heart of all things"—even death. Of course, that doesn't mean it isn't difficult sometimes to find or understand it. However, when the important activities of laughter and play enter into the dying one's experience, we can embrace it. Sherry, R.N., shared this story of one of her young patients:

I once cared for a small, ventilator-dependent child, whose method of happy communication was clicking his tongue against the roof of his mouth or engaging in an eye-blinking contest as he was otherwise totally paralyzed.

We had finished our bedtime routine one cool spring evening and were getting his fuzzy "jammies" on before one last suction. I happened to notice after his jammies were on that he was playing the blinking game quite happily, focusing over my right shoulder, in the direction of his bedroom door. I had closed the door earlier but thought perhaps his parents had returned from their dinner engagement, because the look on his face definitely said, "Mommy and Daddy!"

I turned, expecting to see his parents, but saw no one, and the door was shut. He then started clicking his tongue, still playing the blinking game and ready to burst out in a fit of giggles at any moment. After a brief moment, I had the distinct, overwhelming feeling that I was in the presence of angelic communication with this child. I sat on the floor next to the bed, watching him totally absorbed in joy. After a short time, he began to look at me as if I'd forgotten that last suction before bedtime.

Driving home that night, I was overwhelmed by a premonition of that child's death, though he was healthier at that time than he'd been for some months. I was called to his home three days later to share with his parents his quiet passing.

This experience was a great gift to me—in essence, "Don't fear death!" How could someone so joyfully giggly be fearful? It again became a gift in the sharing of the angel with his mother after his funeral. It seemed to bring a sense of relief, a knowing that he was now with a friend.

As midwives, we come to accept that not all will be lightness and joy during this period of intense life changes. There is pain, grief, and fear that must be acknowledged. There may even be rage, sadness, bitterness, and other negative feelings directed toward us or others. Our role is to accept the dying one as these feelings run their course and never shut off the caring, however we can offer it. Often, this may mean little more than offering a safe place where these feelings can come out. It is easier for the dying one to let go of them if he or she feels he or she hasn't been turned away for having them.

Miriam:

I was once asked to help transfer a new hospice patient from a stretcher to his bed. It took five people on each side to move him. We gently lifted him, taking our time, to keep from causing him undue pain, but our efforts seemed to make little difference. He cried and screamed in pain. We offered pain medication, but he refused. He had been in severe physical pain for several months but refused all medication. He suffered terribly with the slightest touch. It was extremely difficult for the staff to make available the quality of care we were so accustomed to providing.

I was working once again after several days off. The patient in pain had not been assigned to me for care on my shift. As I stood in the doorway, I saw that this man was curled up in a fetal position, his face distraught and pale. I said, "You look so uncomfortable." He replied quickly, "It doesn't matter." I said, "It does matter to me. I care that you are hurting."

I left the room with a determination to speak to the nurse caring for him. I asked her to offer medication one more time. There was something in the way he had said "It doesn't matter" that touched me. It was like understanding he was giving us permission to show we cared. The nurse went in, and he did finally accept our offer of pain medication. We spent the night increasing the morphine that had been prescribed by his physician for so many months.

I was off again for the next few days. When I came back to work, I noticed a man in a wheelchair racing one of the nurses to the end of a hall. His face looked so familiar. Finally, I realized it was him. He shouted to me, "Miriam, I am so glad you're here. There's something I've been wanting to show you." He quickly wheeled into his room and returned with a mandolin. "I used to play this all the time. I can't anymore, but I thought you might like to see it. It's very old." I spent time admiring this beautiful mandolin and listening to his memories of when he played it.

He died a few weeks later. During those few weeks, he called his ex-wife, children, and other estranged family members to his bedside. They spent his last weeks resolving lifelong issues. He died at peace with his family and himself. This man taught me to respect each person's way of coming to terms with their pain. We created a safe place for him to express his anger and fear and acknowledged his pain. We offered a caring, concerned invitation to release him from the pain. We never forced him to do anything. He attended in his own way to the physical pain he suffered and also to the emotional pain that came from his life.

Although it is important to provide a safe place for the dying one to express negative emotions, it may be equally important for the caregiver and family to find appropriate outlets for their volatile feelings. When such feelings arise, conflict and anger may be healthy indicators of the intensity of the labor time. A director of nursing once told us, "If there are issues within a family, illness will amplify them 100-fold." We've yet to find a family without *some* unresolved issues!

Crisis can bring us to a place of honesty within ourselves. So often in our culture, we see anger as an unhealthy emotion rather than a natural one. The reality is that anger and sadness are feelings as genuine as serenity and joyfulness. We simply need to learn how to express these feelings in ways that will be heard.

In *On Death and Dying,* Elisabeth Kübler-Ross discusses the five stages dying people experience: denial, anger, bargaining, depression, and acceptance. In our work, we have seen caregivers experience these same stages of the dying process, sometimes in compressed periods of time. Why do these stages apply to the midwife as well? We must always remember that a part of us dies along with any dying one we love.

The dynamics of a family passing through these stages are sometimes difficult. One of the advantages of participating in a hospice program is that support is provided for these challenges. Trained social service people and spiritual directors can help guide families through the expression of all their emotions. To have an objective third party involved can bring direction and guidance to important decisions caregivers must make.

In an ideal world, many of these decisions would be made ahead of time. Unfortunately, the ideal is not always the reality, and conflict or stress may arise. Fatigue can also play a major role in heightened emotions. Even if you can take just a few minutes a day to create a quiet space within yourself, you will find strength you didn't know you had.

When conflicts do occur, reach out for help before they grow in magnitude. It is sometimes difficult to remember that the center of all your actions *must* be the one who is dying. Save the bulk of your strength for him or her.

Charting the Labor

The charts that follow are a guide to changes in the emotional, physical, and spiritual health of the dying through all the stages of labor. We have also charted many of the changes midwives themselves experience during this challenging time. It is important that the caregiver remember his or her needs as well as the dying one's.

Sometimes it seems there is never enough time to prepare for death adequately or completely. Sometimes, changes occur within hours. It is challenging to respond in a manner that keeps measure with the pace. The charts are formatted so that the caregiver can quickly recognize and follow the progress of labor. When the caregiver can recognize and name changes as they occur, he or she can make better sense of events and respond with the appropriate care.

We hope that the following guide will serve you in your time of need and help you transform fear and pain through love.

STAGE 1: PREACTIVE LABOR

Preactive labor is the initial stage of the dying one's labor preparation. The time spent in this stage may vary greatly—from days to weeks. Remember that your loved one's labor is his or her path to follow, and it has its own sacred schedule. Always take your time.

PHYSICAL LABOR

Physical Changes

- Decreased eating and drinking.

- Change in breathing patterns.
- Increase in pain/confusion/weakness.
- Temperature fluctuations.
- Varied sleeping/waking patterns.
- Heightened sensitivity to sight, sound, smell, and activity.

Support Measures

- Food/fluids as desired.
- Medications to relieve pain and as ordered.
- Cool cloth on body.
- Assistance with physical needs.
- Gentle touching.
- Slow, mindful actions.

EMOTIONAL AND SPIRITUAL LABOR

Emotional and Spiritual Changes

- Withdrawal.
- More frequent crying.
- Fear of being alone, especially at night.
- Restlessness, agitation, and/or anxiety.
- Anger or impatience with loved ones.
- Need to discuss one's own death and others who have died.
- Depression.
- Need to say good-bye to loved ones.
- Completion of will, business closures, funeral plans.
- Acceptance.

Support Measures

- Keep the dying in touch with the time and place.
- Honor dignity by maintaining privacy.
- Begin vigil attendance if appropriate.
- Notify support persons of changes.
- Be honest with patient regarding changes.
- Express how you are feeling.
- Provide calm and reassuring statements.
- Listen quietly.
- Reevaluate extraordinary life-support measures.
- Continue to laugh and play.
- Continue gentle touching.
- Assist with prayer rituals.

CAREGIVERS' CHANGES

Physical, Emotional, and Spiritual Changes

- Fatigue or insomnia.
- Stomach upset.
- Tearfulness.
- Headache.
- Guilt, anger, depression, relief, despair.
- Withdrawal.
- Difficulty balancing loved one's needs with family/home/self.

Support Measures

- Find people who will help with quiet listening, holding, hugging, massage, vigil relief, assistance with care, information.
- Honor all your feelings.

- Nurture yourself—take a bath, nap, walk, exercise, pray, meditate.
- Allow others to help with family and home.
- Honor your grief work—take time for yourself, share feelings and tears.
- Set limits with the loved one.
- Complete funeral arrangements, business matters.

Stage 2: Active Labor

Active labor may be as short as a few hours or as long as a few days.

Physical Labor

Physical Changes

- Skin cooling with mottling.
- Temperature flunctuations.
- Lung congestion.
- Skin color changes.
- Increase in irregular breathing pattern.
- Deterioration in awareness (unable to close eyes, respond verbally, etc.).
- Deterioration of body (odors, loss of bladder and bowel control, etc.).

Support Measures

- Keep warm and dry if cool.
- Use light covers and cool cloth in case of fever.
- Elevate head of bed if tolerated.
- Continue to provide medication or symptom relief.

- Continue familiar comfort measures as tolerated.
- Touch gently.

EMOTIONAL AND SPIRITUAL LABOR

Emotional and Spiritual Changes

- May relax when loved ones are near.
- Restlessness, agitation, and/or anxiety.
- The calmness of acceptance.
- Out-of-body events.
- Fear.
- Intensified sense of spiritual source.

Support Measures

- Continue to talk, touch, and pray.
- Continue comfort, support, and care.
- Talk about beloved people or pets who have died.
- Give permission to let go.
- Trust what your heart directs you to do.

CAREGIVERS' CHANGES

Physical, Emotional, and Spiritual Changes

- Diarrhea, backache, fatigue/insomnia, and loss of appetite.
- Sorrow, fear, and loss.
- Guilt from wanting death to come.
- Numbness.
- Tenderness.
- Closeness to those present.
- Intensified sense of spiritual source.
- Sense of peace or well-being.

Support Measures

- Turn to a support group for continued help.
- Ask yourself, What do I want or need?
- Honor your feelings; give yourself room to experience the negative as well as the positive.
- Contact those who provide spiritual support.
- Nurture yourself—take a bath, nap, walk, exercise, meditate, pray.

STAGE 3: DEATH

The moment of death is a long one. Just as the moment of birth, it contains within it an eternity of meanings and sensations. It is the time of our last good-byes.

PHYSICAL LABOR

Physical Changes

- A need to push, as if birthing.
- Breathing will gradually stop.
- Pulse is not present.
- Skin color changes to gray.
- May have involuntary loss of stool or urine.
- Mouth and eyes may remain open.

Support Measures

- Remove tubes.
- Cleanse and prepare the body for funeral home.

EMOTIONAL AND SPIRITUAL LABOR

Emotional and Spiritual Changes

- Complete disconnection from physical life.

Support Measures

- Tell him or her good-bye in whatever way possible.
- Pay tribute to his or her life through spoken words and prayer ritual.
- If you are able, stay with the body until the funeral home arrives; if desired, accompany the body to the funeral home.
- Honor dignity by keeping the body covered, gently touching, cleansing the body carefully.

CAREGIVERS' CHANGES

Physical, Emotinoal, and Spiritual Changes

- Fatigue/insomnia.
- Relief of physical discomforts.
- Variety of feelings expressed through screaming, pounding, walking, being silent, moaning or touching, kissing, hugging, lying beside, or standing by loved one.

Support Measures

- Honor your needs for rest, time alone, and time away.
- Listen, hold, and hug quietly.
- Allow feelings to surface.
- Accept assistance if that is what you want.

- If you desire, ask for time alone with the one who has died to bathe or dress the body.
- Pray, meditate, quietly reflect.

Note: Each state has its own required protocol following death, but most are similar. For instance, in Oregon, a hospice team nurse may be able to pronounce the death. The medical examiner would then be notified by the hospice nurse, who would also give the required biographical information. The medical examiner can then release the body to the funeral home by phone; there is no need for the medical examiner to go to the home. At this point, the hospice nurse can make the necessary calls notifying the physician, pharmacy, medical equipment supplier, hospice team, and anybody else appropriate. The family would be asked if they want a home visit, and they would be encouraged to contact anyone whose presence is needed before the funeral home representative is called. The family would be encouraged to take as much time as they need to say their good-byes.

5

Management of Pain and Other Symptoms

THE WEAVER

Where will you go when your days are passing slow
And life is running out of laughter
And who will you be when your mind has set you free
And shadows are lost inside your sorrow
And how can you find that you have peace of mind
When all your dreams are in tomorrow
How could it be that you have never seen
The pain you bought was only borrowed
And you never tried to find if you could fly
And now your wings are torn and broken
Living on the run wasn't any fun
These words you once thought were never spoken
For ink upon the sand could never once demand
To last through sun and hope and winter

MANAGEMENT OF PAIN AND OTHER SYMPTOMS

And you never knew that the pictures that you drew
Were to give a face to all this madness
You and I were one as we walked in the sun
And hung our stars upon the rainbow
And now you understand in the weaving of your hand
Your breath is all you need to follow

—JANET PETERSON

When individuals discuss their fear of dying, they invariably cite the pain involved. The perception of pain in the dying process has recently become a political question as well, with many activists and health care professionals advocating legalized assisted suicide as a way for the dying to minimize this pain. The voters in the State of Oregon approved a referendum legalizing assisted suicide in 1994, although the measure has yet to be enacted while it is debated in the court system. In the meantime, signatures are being collected in states around the country for similar referendums. Assisted suicide is being increasingly advocated and practiced by the dying well before the onset of preactive labor, in many cases so that patients can "die with dignity."

Before the vote in Oregon was held, a report was issued from a series of community meetings involving several hundred voters: "Request for Physician-Assisted Death: How Will You Vote?" In the executive summary of the report, the concern for uncontrolled pain and suffering was held to be a major issue for voters seeking to resolve their views.

Although we cannot presume to judge any person's choice regarding their path to death, we do know that many of the public assumptions about pain are based on misperceptions. Despite common belief, crippling physical pain is not a universal experience for the dying. Recent studies examining the last forty-eight hours of life and our own experience suggest that even the *majority* of the dying do not have any symptoms of severe discomfort (Doyle et al., 1993). As early as the turn of the century, the medical establishment concluded that only in a minority of cases did death involve notable suffering. The pioneering work of Sir William Osler still provides enlightenment in this area:

> I have careful records of about 500 deathbeds, studied particularly with reference to the modes of death and the sensations of the dying. The latter alone concerns us here. Ninety suffered bodily pain or distress of one sort or another, eleven showed mental apprehension, two positive terror, one expressed spiritual exaltation, one bitter remorse. The great majority gave no signs one way or the other; like their birth, their death was a sleep and a forgetting. (circa 1910; quoted in Doyle et al., 1993)

We deal with another misconception when we say that for nearly all who *do* suffer physical pain, both traditional and naturopathic medicines and practices can control suffering, if not completely eliminate pain.

Finally, we question the assumption that anyone who would experience in full the natural process of dying lacks dignity in any way. It is true that the dying must surrender to forces far beyond their control during labor and may lose control of bodily functions. Yet the woman in childbirth undergoes nearly the identical process, and none would think of calling her "undignified." In fact, we feel that the person who becomes open to the challenge of labor—whether in birth or death—has achieved the highest level of dignity in human life.

Saying all this, we do not wish to imply for a moment that pain is a minor or insignificant issue. Because it *is* so important, we have resolved to treat the topic separately in this chapter. In fact, we feel many who advocate suicide as a way to avoid pain may often overlook certain kinds of pain that accompany the process of dying. In addition to physical pain, the dying can also experience emotional and spiritual pain as well. In their exclusive focus on physical pain, many advocates may not recognize or respond to these sources of suffering in those they are trying to help. We believe that in many cases non-physical sources of pain can be more serious and in need of support than physical sources. In the current political debate, many have questioned whether those diagnosed with a terminal illness might commit suicide during a temporary episode of depression, long before they have actual symptoms and long before they have had time to come to peace with family and friends.

It is our feeling that most of the perceptions of pain are based on the fear of the unknown. Our purpose in writing this book is to describe fully and to honor the labor of dying so that readers can make informed choices regarding their options. In the remainder of this chapter, we describe the established and proven methods hospice care professionals use to comfort and support the dying and caregivers. Certainly, many who are overcome with anxiety when first faced with the prospect of labor, pain, and dying are relieved and can let go of their fear when they are convinced that an effective network of medical and traditional caregivers and therapies exists to help them. These measures have withstood the test of time, and no professional in the field of dying would allow any patient to suffer needlessly, even for a moment. At the end of this chapter, we include a full list of conventional and alternative measures and medications used to alleviate suffering. We also include naturopathic therapies.

The Right Care at the Right Time

During active labor, a dying person needs total care. He or she will require assistance in all areas of living, even decisions concerning comfort and support. This takes enormous energy on the part of family and other caregivers. Hospice care teams exist nationwide to assist the dying and lighten the burden for caregivers.

Of all the caregiver's contacts with the hospice team during the active phase of the dying, it is the relationship between the physician and the family that is most important. The ability to provide comfort measures using prescription drugs and some medical or naturopathic treatments, not to mention admission to a hospice or other care facility, becomes dependent on effective communication within this relationship, typically mediated by a nurse. With this in mind, we are able to give an idea of how a hospice care team functions to provide the required or desired care for the dying one.

The nurse becomes the designated person to communicate with the physician in addition to the caregivers chosen for or by the dying one. The nurse, in conjunction with the dying one and caregivers, provides the information to the physician on the current symptoms needing attention. A coordinated plan of care is then possible. The appropriate medications and treatments can then be initiated by this health care team.

This communication model brings order to the complex design of care management. The overwhelming majority of people who die do so with others assisting them.

Some people may have only one person present with them throughout this time. Others may have several friends or their family providing care. There may exist another layer of caregivers if a person has entered a care facility. Because the inherent expectation is that the patient's body will be deteriorating and that this deterioration will be uncomfortable, unpredictable, and challenging for some, it is crucial that the dying one and caregivers have access to assistance at any time day or night.

Hospice teams provide a twenty-four-hour telephone number for these times. It is remarkable what a difference a simple fifteen-minute telephone conversation can make. It can decrease emotional stress, anxiety, and suffering for the caregiver as well as the dying one. Literally millions of telephone calls have been made to hospice nurses in the late evening or early morning hours by caregivers in need. The caregiver may begin by saying something like "Something is wrong. I'm not sure what to do, but Grandpa stopped eating yesterday. He only took a sip or two of water today. He can't seem to swallow anymore, so we just moisten his mouth. He's not even waking up and getting out of bed. His breathing is different. Sometimes he stops breathing altogether for a while. What should I do?"

The nurse responding will take time to ask questions, listen to the answers, and provide guidance. The conversation might go something like this (N, nurse; C, caregiver):

N: Does Grandpa talk to you anymore?

C: No.

N: Does he show signs he is hurting by moaning, frowning, or any other way?

C: No.

N: Does he work at breathing or does he seem to be anxious or restless during the times he stops breathing?

C: Yes, he tries to sit up, so we propped him up with pillows and that seemed to help.

N: When was the last time he urinated?

C: It was a few hours ago and not very much. We have to use the adult-size pads now that he can't reach or hold his urinal. We change his pad every couple of hours if he needs it and keep him clean and dry.

N: Your grandpa's body has changed a great deal in the past forty-eight hours. He's gone from talking, eating, drinking, using his urinal, and being able to get out of bed to not being able to do any of those things. Plus he is having to work at breathing. I am glad to hear he is not having pain. You are taking excellent care of him by keeping his mouth moist, propping him up in bed to breathe more easily, changing his pads, and keeping him clean and dry. You have described many of the signs indicating that his death is approaching. Do you believe your grandpa is dying?

C: Yes, this is a lot like Grandma when she died, except she was in the hospital when she died.

A discussion on the signs and symptoms of approaching death would normally follow. Time would be allowed for the caregiver to talk about how all of these changes are affecting her. The nurse would then ask if the caregiver was still able to continue to provide care. If the caregiver decided he or she could not, a discussion would then follow concerning available options, resulting in a plan the caregiver could agree with and carry out. The nurse might also inquire if appropriate family and friends have been notified of any profound changes. Additional instructions on comfort measures might include the use of oxygen, medications to assist breathing, and choices of medical equipment.

A decision should be made to determine how soon a nurse is needed to come to the home. Some might prefer that the nurse rush to the home immediately following the telephone conversation. Others may request to have a nurse follow up at a later time that day or the next, unless the comfort measures are clearly not sufficient.

This scenario illustrates a relatively uncomplicated change of a person's condition to the active stage of dying and the hospice response. Obviously, other more challenging events can occur. Nonetheless, within the current structure of hospice, whether at home or in a facility, there is a way to problem solve any change or crisis as it occurs. The symptoms causing distress are important to attend to as they occur. These times of profound change create a stress response within the caregiver and the dying one. Anxiety is decreased by at least 50 percent when we are able to seek a competent response from others, according to research on anxiety reduction techniques (Irving, 1974). This reduction in anxiety affects everyone in the situation: the caregiver, the dying one, and the nurse.

Responding to Symptoms Using Conventional and Naturopathic Principles

We share a belief that a wide variety of options, both conventional and naturopathic, exist to bring comfort and healing to those in need. For us it is a combination of these two types of medicine that assist the healing process. However, for any treatment to be effective the patient must believe in it. As Dr. Bernie Siegel says in *Love, Medicine & Miracles,* "The belief systems of physicians and patients interact, but the patients' bodies respond directly to their own beliefs, not the doctors'."

Naturopathic medicine is based on a concept of healing that employs natural means of preventing and treating disease. Because of the gentle nature of naturopathic treatments, they are very effective when used during the dying process, and the treatment approach is very individualized.

The focus of a conventional approach to hospice care is on providing comfort and support measures, which is achieved through the use of prescription drugs in the management of pain and other symptoms.

We encourage you to use the information in this chapter about major symptoms and their treatment at the time of dying to initiate dialogue with the hospice team or simply to generate treatment ideas. Of course, working with professionals is crucial. It is not possible to describe exactly how each person might react or respond to the various treatments suggested, since each person is unique. What is important to remember is that generations of hospice teams have been gathering knowledge and experience to bring the highest quality of care to patients. What remains constant is the communication among the hospice team, assessing each change as it happens, developing a plan of responding with comfort and support, and continually evaluating the effectiveness of treatments.

Main Physical Symptoms Causing Discomfort During the Active Phase of Dying

SYMPTOMS: According to the *Oxford Textbook of Palliative Care* (Doyle et al.), the main physical symptoms causing discomfort during the active labor of dying for some

132

people are restlessness, anxiety, agitation, confusion and/ or delirium; fever; hemorrhaging; sweating; nausea and/ or vomiting; pain; seizures; shortness of breath; noisy, moist breathing; urinary/bowel incontinence or retention; jerking, twitching and plucking, that is picking at air or sheets. Most hospice responses focus on these symptoms.

The dying one may exhibit one or more of these symptoms, and the intensity may be slight or severe. The question to keep at the forefront when giving care is "does this action provide relief?" We list fourteen of the most common physical symptoms we observe in the active phase of dying.

PRESCRIPTION DRUGS: How a medication is given to a patient becomes a major issue when the person is no longer able to swallow. Each medication listed in the following tables is available for administration without swallowing. Medications can be absorbed through several different routes. They can be placed in the mouth (sublingual) where they are absorbed through the mucosal lining; or in the rectum (suppository), or on the skin (transdermal). There may be placement of a needle into a blood vessel (intravenous), under the skin (subcutaneous), or finally by placement of a catheter into the epidural space of the spine. The decision about which route to use becomes dependent on the capability of the caregiver to properly administer it as well as the dying one's preference.

Health care professionals will discuss the available options during the decision-making process. The ultimate goal is to deliver the medication in a manner that will ensure the greatest benefit.

NATUROPATHIC TREATMENTS—A FEW APPROACHES: BOTANICAL MEDICINE uses plants as medicinal agents. Herbs balance and relieve the symptoms that occur during the dying process. They can be given in the form of tinctures, salves, or suppositories. Naturopathic physicians are trained as herbalists. When using herbs, it is vital to understand the pharmacological mechanisms of plants and their interactions with other medications that are being prescribed.

HOMEOPATHY uses remedies that stimulate the body's own healing power using a holistic approach. By giving a diluted, potentized substance or drug you in effect are waking up the body to respond to a particular symptom. Homeopathics come from a variety of plants and chemical substances. They are given in liquid or pellet form. Extensive training is required to apply the principles of homeopathy to the dying.

BACH FLOWER REMEDIES are liquid extracts of flowers that are used to facilitate emotional well-being and the connection between the mind and the body. When used during the dying process, they help balance the emotional and psychological stresses. They are simple to use and can be given in liquid form. Bach Flower remedies are used orally, applied directly to the area of discomfort, or placed in bath water. You will need to consult a naturopathic physician for prescribing of specific botanicals, homeopathics, and Bach Flower remedies.

NUTRITION As someone is dying, his or her body requires much less nutritionally than before, so it is important to optimize the quality of fluids and supplements. Powdered supplements, free of preservatives and dyes, provide a higher caloric intake as well as vitamins and minerals.

HYDROTHERAPY is the therapeutic use of water in the treatment of disease, involving the use of alternating hot and cold water, compresses, wraps, baths, and poultices. In the dying process hydrotherapy stimulates relief of symptoms and relaxation by enhancing oxygenation and circulation of the blood and lymph fluid. Excellent information about hydrotherapy is available from the book, *Lecture on Naturopathic Hydrotherapy* by W. Boyle and Andre Saine.

PHYSICAL INTERVENTIONS THAT PROVIDE COMFORT: Foley catheters, oxygen therapy, egg crate mattresses, and massage to maintain skin integrity.

SYMPTOM: Restlessness, Agitation, Anxiety, Confusion and/or Delirium

PRESCRIPTION DRUGS AND NATUROPATHIC MEDICATIONS: Ativan, Xanax, Haldol, Valium

Only one of these drugs will be used at a time. Botanicals, homeopathy, and Bach Flower remedies are appropriate and should be prescribed by a specialist.

CONVENTIONAL AND NATUROPATHIC APPROACHES: The following hydrotherapy treatments will sedate the dying one. *Warming sheet packs:* Wrap their body in a moist sheet. Place a dry blanket on the outside of the moist sheet. Leave this on for twenty minutes. *Neutral bath:* The water temperature should be 92°–97°F. Place the dying one in the bath. They will need someone to attend to them.

COMMENTS: Confusion, paranoia and/or hallucinations may be evident. A person is noisy, restless, and even combative. Attempts to reason with the patient make the agitation worse. Safety is a primary issue. It is important to note that the patient will need someone with them at all times. A calm environment is helpful. Providing clear, simple instructions in a quiet, firm manner is desirable. It is extremely challenging when the anxiety and agitation are profound. The more severe the symptoms are, the more likely that placement into a twenty-four-hour care facility will be advised if the caregivers within a home setting are unable to cope with the care needs. Use of medication to treat the behavior is a standard response by the health care team. Very often other symptoms such as pain, dehydration, or respiratory distress are part of the scenario and will be assessed at this time. The hospice team will discuss options with the physician, and a plan of care will be implemented to meet the person's need.

SYMPTOM: Fever

PRESCRIPTION DRUGS AND NATUROPATHIC MEDICATIONS: Acetaminophen or aspirin

One of these drugs will be ordered. Botanicals, homeopathy, and Bach Flower remedies are appropriate and should be prescribed by a specialist.

CONVENTIONAL AND NATUROPATHIC APPROACHES: The following hydrotherapy treatments will assist in decreasing the fever. *Tepid sponge bath:* The water temperature should be 81°–92°F. Gently sponge the entire body. *Evaporating sheet wrap:* Wrap the dying one's body in a moistened warm sheet. Apply friction through the sheet and let the sheet cool. Be careful not to decrease the temperature quickly.

COMMENTS: The majority of fevers seen at the end of life arise because of the brain's inability to regulate temperature. These fevers at times do not respond to the medications listed. Cool cloths, light coverings, fans, and so on are more likely to provide comfort.

SYMPTOM: Hemorrhaging

PRESCRIPTION DRUGS AND NATUROPATHIC MEDICATIONS: Ativan, Xanax, Valium (see **Pain** for additional medication)

One of these drugs will be ordered by a doctor. Botanicals, homeopathy, and Bach Flower remedies are appropriate and should be prescribed by a specialist.

CONVENTIONAL AND NATUROPATHIC TREATMENT APPROACHES: Apply *cold compress or ice pack* over the area of bleeding and cover with wool for twenty minutes.

COMMENTS: Some diseases may result in external bleeding. This can be very frightening for all present. Remain with the person to provide comfort and reassurance. Place him or her in a comfortable position (i.e., upright on side if bleeding from the mouth). If bleeding is elsewhere apply pressure to area. Should bleeding occur internally or externally, there may be a profound increase in localized pain. Seek assistance for pain management from the hospice team.

SYMPTOM: Perspiring

PRESCRIPTION DRUGS AND NATUROPATHIC MEDICATIONS: Botanicals, homeopathy, and Bach Flower remedies are appropriate and should be prescribed by a specialist.

CONVENTIONAL AND NATUROPATHIC APPROACHES: *Tepid sponge bath* (see **Fever**).

COMMENTS: Change the clothing and linens frequently. Use terry cloth bath-size towels to absorb sweat and decrease the need for complete bed changes. Clothing should be easy to take off and on. Many people choose to cut shirts in the back and place ties or Velcro fasteners to secure the neck, similar to a hospital gown.

SYMPTOM: Nausea and/or Vomiting

PRESCRIPTION DRUGS AND NATUROPATHIC MEDICATIONS: Compazine, Ativan, Benadryl, Reglan suppository, Inapsine, Phenergan, and/or Vistaril; placement of nasogastric tube to suction

One of these drugs may be ordered at a time. Botanicals, homeopathy, and Bach Flower remedies are appropriate and should be prescribed by a specialist.

CONVENTIONAL AND NATUROPATHIC APPROACHES: *Castor oil pack:* Cover cotton cloth with Castor oil and place on abdomen. Cover with wool and leave on for two hours.

COMMENTS: If nausea and vomiting are continuous, provide medication on a continuous basis. The medications listed are used in order. Compazine is used with moderate nausea/vomiting. The other medications are implemented if the symptoms are severe and do not respond to Compazine. The health care professional will be checking for abdominal obstruction (i.e., no abdominal sounds present, abdominal distention). An obstruction can be treated by inserting a tube through the nasal passage and into the stomach, which provides relief by drawing out stomach contents and relieving the pressure. This procedure is uncomfortable. The choice not to insert a tube is also an option. The treatment choice relies not only upon the physician's expertise, but also upon the dying one's caregivers' desire. Another supportive measure would be to start increasing pain medication (see **Pain**). At this point all oral medications, food, or drink would be held. Oral care becomes increasingly important.

SYMPTOM: Decreased Eating and Drinking

COMMENTS: The dying one's ability to eat and drink is diminishing during this time. It may be impossible to administer oral medications. Other routes to deliver medications will be used. Many medications will be discontinued unless they provide relief of pain and discomfort. The lungs may have excess fluid. The collection of body fluids within the body causes bloating and swelling. These areas may be taut and painful. Intravenous fluids would not be a comfort measure at this time. The reason for this is that the body is unable to circulate the body fluids. The addition of intravenous fluids would result in increasing edema, thus increasing the pain. The use of intravenous fluids needs to be carefully evaluated. The question to ask once again is, Who am I comforting: myself or the dying one? Recall what the dying one told you he or she wanted during his or her final days. Food and fluids need to be offered but never forced. The guideline of what to provide will always be, Does the action provide relief?

SYMPTOM: Pain

PRESCRIPTION DRUGS AND NATUROPATHIC MEDICATIONS: Oxycodone, morphine, Dilaudid, and/or Duragesic Transdermal System (fentynl)

One of these drugs will be ordered. Botanicals, homeopathy, and Bach Flower remedies are appropriate and should be prescribed by a specialist.

CONVENTIONAL AND NATUROPATHIC APPROACHES: *Moist cool compresses:* Apply moist compress to area of pain and cover with wool or flannel. *Neutral bath* (see **Restlessness, Agitation, Anxiety, Confusion and/or Delirium**) for directions. *Poultice:* Apply a hot, soft, moist material directly to the skin and cover with plastic, then wool. Poultice substances may be used with herbs, mustard, shredded carrots, or potatoes.

COMMENTS: Pain is a primary issue for many people. The active phase of dying is an even larger challenge for some. A person experiences increased pain because of the disease process (tumor growth, internal bleeding, etc.); skin breakdown; dehydration affecting the oral cavity, causing a dry and sore mouth; and/or fungal or topical skin infections. The support team will need to provide ongoing assessment of where the pain is and what measures are needed. There will be a continuous evaluation of the measures implemented. A dying person does not need to endure excruciating pain. Pain can be minimized to a tolerable if not pain-free level. The use of the above-mentioned medications and treatments have proved to be effective in reducing or eliminating the perception of pain. It is also helpful to use music and imagery in combination with medication. Keep room environment quiet.

SYMPTOM: Skin Wounds

PRESCRIPTION DRUGS AND NATUROPATHIC MEDICATIONS: Medicated creams and gels (e.g., zinc oxide ointments, creams, gels or sprays, bag balm, baza cream)

Botanicals, homeopathy, application of herbal salves (ie., vit E, A, calendula) and Bach Flower remedies are appropriate and should be prescribed by a specialist.

CONVENTIONAL AND NATUROPATHIC APPROACHES: Egg-carton, Geomatt or alternating pressure mattress. Apply dressings to absorb wound drainage and provide protective barriers.

COMMENTS: Skin breakdown is caused by immobility and the general loss of body tissue. A program involves keeping the skin clean and dry, turning and repositioning every one to two hours, massaging with lotion, keeping linens and clothing clean and dry. Administer lotions, medication ointments, and/or dressings for the conditions noted above. Care also provides the opportunity to continue touch. Often, touching brings the greatest comfort and is ultimately the healing needed for the heart for both the caregiver and care receiver. As a person enters into the active labor of dying, complete body care may not be possible. For some, the process would be too uncomfortable. Be attentive to how care is being received. The person may not be able to communicate verbally. It is important to let your other senses take over. Look at how the person is breathing during turns, observe facial expressions for wincing or grimacing, whether the arms and legs are relaxed, and listen for moaning or groaning. These are clues to the person's pain perception. The measures to consider if these responses are present are to provide additional pain medication; a softer, more gentle touch; decrease the physical interventions; remember to use a soothing tone to verbalize your actions. There are several people within the hospice team capable of teaching nonexperts how to provide the physical care a person needs: home health aides provide bathing and personal grooming; physical or occupational therapists may teach or provide equipment to make tasks more comfortable and easier to do; and nurses may follow up on teaching or doing the more complex tasks of dressing changes, colostomy care, and teaching as related to comfort and support in the dying process. Often less pain medication is required when a person is being provided care in a competent, gentle manner.

Skin

SYMPTOM: Herpes

PRESCRIPTION DRUGS AND NATUROPATHIC MEDICATIONS: Acyclovir/Benadryl/Xylocaine ointment

One of these or a combination will be ordered. Botanicals, homeopathy, and Bach Flower remedies are appropriate and should be prescribed by a specialist.

SYMPTOM: Fungal Infections

PRESCRIPTION DRUGS AND NATUROPATHIC MEDICATIONS: Monistat cream or Micatin powder; Botanicals, homeopathy, and Bach Flower remedies are appropriate and should be prescribed by a specialist.

SYMPTOM: Topical Infections

PRESCRIPTION DRUGS AND NATUROPATHIC MEDICATIONS: Medicated antibiotic ointments (e.g., Neosporin)

Botanicals, homeopathy, and Bach Flower remedies are appropriate and should be prescribed by a specialist.

COMMENTS: Each skin condition (wounds, herpes, and fungal and topical infections) requires the application of the appropriate prescription drug treatment, and naturopathic treatment as directed. Apply to the infected area on an as-needed basis. At times, it may be uncomfortable for the dying one if he or she must be turned and repositioned. Provide pain medication prior to repositioning if needed to ensure comfort during the procedure.

SYMPTOM: Sore Mouth/Candidiasis

PRESCRIPTION DRUGS AND NATUROPATHIC MEDICATIONS: Sore mouth: Mylanta/Benadryl/viscous Xylocaine liquid, or nystatin. One or more of these drugs will be prescribed.

Botanical solutions, suspensions or topical creams, homeopathy, and Bach Flower remedies are appropriate and should be prescribed by a specialist.

COMMENTS: As the person enters into the active phase of dying, the body fluids diminish, the gums may crack and become inflamed, and food debris and dried sputum can coat the mouth. The person will no longer be able to brush his or her teeth. Care must be given. Moisten the mouth often with ice chips or a water aerosol spray to replace lost saliva. Keep lips covered with a protective coating. Other conditions such as a sore mouth or candidiasis (thrush, a fungal disease) may already exist or suddenly occur. The health care team will assist in determining the appropriate medication and/or treatment.

SYMPTOM: Seizures

PRESCRIPTION DRUGS AND NATUROPATHIC MEDICATIONS: Ativan, Valium, Dilantin, Phenobarbital

One or more of these drugs will be prescribed. Botanicals, homeopathy, and Bach Flower remedies are appropriate and should be prescribed by a specialist.

CONVENTIONAL AND NATUROPATHIC APPROACHES: Follow fever treatment protocol.

COMMENTS: During a seizure, remain with the person. The focus of care is to keep that person safe. Lower him to the floor if he is in a chair. Pad the railings if he is in a hospital bed. Keep him on his side if possible to avoid inhalation of vomit should that occur during the seizure. Reassure him verbally. Confusion and disorientation may follow a seizure. Some seizures do not involve the whole body. If this is the case, it may be entirely appropriate for the person to remain seated. Quietly observe his physical responses as well as the duration of the seizure. The hospice nurse should be notified as soon as possible to provide assistance in notifying the physician for medication and treatment orders.

SYMPTOM: Shortness of Breath (Dyspnea)

PRESCRIPTION DRUGS AND NATUROPATHIC MEDICATIONS: Morphine, Ativan, Xanax, oxygen therapy

One or more of these drugs will be prescribed. Botanicals, homeopathy, and Bach Flower remedies are appropriate and should be prescribed by a specialist.

CONVENTIONAL AND NATUROPATHIC APPROACHES: *Compresses to the chest* (see **Pain** section). *Steam inhalation* with essential oils added can also be used for a poultice to chest (see **Pain** section).

COMMENTS: During the active phase of dying, a person may experience dramatic changes in the ability to breathe. The body is quite weak at this point. Fluid may be building up in the lungs of some. Others may simply be too weak to move the fluid out through coughing and swallowing. The respiratory rate may increase and become labored. The hands, feet, arms, and legs may be bluish, cool, and/or mottled. Should a person exhibit these symptoms, the hospice response would be to provide the medications ordered by the physician. There may be a need for more than one medication. It is not uncommon for morphine and Ativan or Xanax to be used at the same time to control the symptoms. Oxygen is helpful for some. Others cannot tolerate having the nasal cannula placed in the nose. The medications can be administered effectively to compensate for oxygen should the cannula not be tolerated by the dying one. It is vital to provide a calm environment and emotional support as the shortness of breath is happening.

SYMPTOM: Noisy, Moist Breathing

PRESCRIPTION DRUGS AND NATUROPATHIC MEDICATIONS: Scopolomine, atropine; oral suctioning (if part of normal treatment)

One of these drugs may be prescribed. Botanicals, homeopathy, and Bach Flower remedies are appropriate and should be prescribed by a specialist.

CONVENTIONAL AND NATUROPATHIC APPROACHES: *Steam inhalation* and essential oils. *Poultices to chest* (see **Pain** section).

COMMENTS: Many have termed this sound the "death rattle." It is simply an inability to clear secretions from the back of the throat. It is important to start the medications at the onset of this symptom. They stop secretions but do not dry up what is already present. This noise is generally more uncomfortable for the listener than for the dying one. It typically occurs during the latter portion of the active phase of dying. For a few, it can contribute to an increase in respiratory distress. See **Shortness of Breath** for suggested treatment. Oral suctioning is appropriate for those secretions reached by a suction tube placed into the mouth and the back of the throat. Suctioning into the lungs is not generally recommended for this symptom as it tends to stimulate the mucosal lining in the lungs to secrete additional fluids. This would then increase the need to suction more frequently. It is an uncomfortable and invasive treatment to place suction tubing into the lungs. Done frequently, it would no longer be considered a comfort measure unless it has been part of their treatment prior to the active phase of dying. Using medication to stop the production of secretions, naturopathic approaches positioning the head of the bed at a 45° to 90° angle, and providing measures if needed for respiratory distress are the optimal comfort choices.

SYMPTOM: Urinary/Bowel Care (Incontinence or Retention)

PRESCRIPTION DRUGS AND NATUROPATHIC MEDICATIONS: Botanicals, homeopathy, and Bach Flower remedies are appropriate and should be prescribed by a specialist.

CONVENTIONAL AND NATUROPATHIC APPROACHES: Foley catheter placement.

COMMENTS: A person who is dying becomes progressively weaker. Assistance begins by physically assisting the patient to the bathroom. It then becomes necessary to assist the patient from the bed to a bedside commode.

Finally, a person is unable to get out of bed. All care is then done at the bedside. Urinary and bowel care is a fundamental need. The goal is to keep the skin clean and dry. Some people use adult-sized pads to keep the urine and/or stool contained. These pads must be frequently checked and changed. If skin problems already exist, note suggestions under **Skin Wounds**. Some people require and/or desire the placement of a Foley catheter. Therefore, the hospice nurse/physician will place a tube into the bladder through the urethra. The flexible, rubber-type catheter will stay in the bladder, where urine is stored. The open end is then connected to a drainage bag. The caregivers are taught how to empty the drainage bag and keep the area clean and dry. As always, cleansing with soap and water and keeping the skin dry are part of the care plan. Should diarrhea or constipation be a problem during this time, a plan of response will be determined. The ultimate goal continues to be one of comfort. The caregiver, dying one, nurse, and/or physician will determine the best course of action.

SYMPTOM: Jerking, Twitching, and Plucking (picking at the air and covers)

PRESCRIPTION DRUGS AND NATUROPATHIC MEDICATIONS: Phenobarbitol, Valium, Ativan, Xanax, or Haldol

One of these drugs will be ordered. Botanicals, homeopathy and Bach Flower remedies are appropriate and should be prescribed by a specialist.

CONVENTIONAL AND NATUROPATHIC APPROACHES: *Moist sheet pack* (see **Pain** section).

COMMENTS: Generally, the symptoms are tolerable if they occur occasionally. Should they occur frequently and/or cause undue stress, the physician is typically notified. A change in medication thought to be causing the symptom could occur. If there is another source, one of the medications listed would be given to resolve the symptom. Part of the body's response to the end stage of the dying process is a shutting down of the control centers of the brain. These symptoms are a result of these changes.

Jan is a naturopathic physician, and she now practices its philosophy of care. Her story of her practice of naturopathy with the remarkable Alex belongs here:

Jan:

I recently had the incredible opportunity to apply naturopathic principles to Alex, a five-year-old girl whom I cared for from initial diagnosis until the death moment. She and her family embraced the complementary approach of health care. They used aggressive chemotherapy and radiation along with botanicals, homeopathics, Bach Flower remedies, hydrotherapy, and art therapy. As a naturopathic medical student and registered nurse, I had a unique opportunity to work side by side with her doctors and the hospice care team.

I consulted with many practitioners of different medical backgrounds. Together we developed a treatment approach that fit the needs of this family. As her breathing became difficult and labored, we used many different treatment modalities. We combined botanicals with a continuous morphine drip. Hydrotherapy treatments allowed her family to participate actively in treatments that provided comfort. We used essential oils in the steam inhalation therapy. For her parents we prescribed homeopathy and Bach Flower remedies. Therapeutic touch eased her difficult breathing. As she lay close to death, we would sing to her and tell her stories about when she was small. We spoke to her of an image of a beautiful butterfly that was being released from the cocoon that was now her body. We cared for her spirit and her physical body. Her mom and dad intuitively knew when to add new things and when to stop. We trusted this process. We trusted the gifts that traditional and nontraditional medicine brought to this little one. A bridge between two worlds of medicine that are sometimes seemingly miles apart was built through Alexandra Rathburn-Ellis.

6

Rituals for Remembering

When someone dies, not only does a life come to an end, but so do the hopes and dreams that the person once shared with others. The practice of ritual and ceremony before and after death help to close the circle of life at the proper time and bring healing. In this chapter, we will share stories of ritual that have been part of our own hospice nursing practices. Rather than focus on the well-established rituals of the major religious paths, which can presumably be discussed with your pastoral care provider, we focus on the private ways we have found that families have marked the passage of the dying shortly before and after death.

Rituals are part of our everyday life. A certain routine as we begin our day, a special prayer said with children at bedtime—these are rituals. Whether informal or formal, rituals bring life back into balance. We are given the ability to quiet our minds and reconnect to our spiritual source within. We share a part of ourselves with others and the world when we share a ritual.

Through rituals a holy space is created to accomplish all these things. Many religious or spiritual ceremonies derive their power from symbolizing an event or person from the past, creating a time for reflection to honor the memory. Those who designed these ceremonies understood that the past connects one to the present; through the repetition of ritual, the present also connects to the future. Remembering brings an understanding of who you are.

A Time for Grief

In caring for the dying one, much of your time and energy goes into that process. Following the death, there is suddenly a huge void and a sense of not being grounded. One moment you may feel relief and the next you may feel a deep sense of loss and sadness.

Following a death, give yourself time to honor your grief. Life may never be the same, but it does continue. Who you are will be forever affected by the experience of death, and your grief may at times feel unbearable. Fully experiencing your grief may be one of the most powerful lessons of your life. Suffering and joy create the fine balance we call living.

The rituals following death are experiences of completion; they are about saying good-bye not only to the one who has died, but also to what *was*. These good-byes make it possible to feel the full range of your emotions and to create a space to welcome what the future will bring.

The following story offers a powerful example of ritual providing a space of peace for the surviving caregiver. Because the storyteller provides such an honest, beautiful account of the complete experience of the midwife—from anxiety to chaos to tenderness to grief—we have included her story in its entirety.

Georgeene:

The dying had been hard. It had lasted for ten months, and it was still too soon, too young. Don was only thirty-eight. He was leaving a six-year-old son and a daughter not yet three. The dying was too sense-less. How had AIDS come into our lives? If he knew, he couldn't share that final guilt.

The diagnosis caused two things to happen: it gal-vanized his family and it threw me out of the picture. There was no more husband to plan with, to share with. There was an invalid, someone with a "termi-nal" illness to care for. Except for the rare occasion, that's how he thought of himself. A dying man. It was true. The disease was progressing quickly. My role now had become one of pure management. How to relieve his burdens? How to maintain an income? How to keep the children's world in a semblance of normality? How to organize? There was never enough time to act; it was happening too fast. Changes were coming at the speed of light. None of them positive. React, react, react. Decisions had to be made within hours, never the luxury of days. A month could mean a lifetime. All the while, the man who had been my partner, who shared my memories of the last eighteen years, the only person in the world to whom I could communicate years of inside jokes with a glance, was retreating farther and farther from our life, from the defining world of work he had been forced to give up, from his children who made too much noise and represented too much loss, and from me, the person who no longer had the time or energy to be his strength.

His family became his strength. Though not living in town, his parents were always there, torn apart but vigilant at his side whenever a crisis loomed. And his brother, the priest. They had been at odds over something most of their lives. Not much in common. Now Don's "little brother" was offering peace, humor, and personal healing. And his two sisters. Just always there. Lives in disarray. Living in hospital corridors and over telephone lines to be beside him. And the rest of his family: aunts, uncles, cousins. Confused, not knowing what to do or say, but never abandoning him.

I couldn't be a part of that. A huge part of me was dying, but at the same time I had my family to maintain. My family became myself and my children. A family of survivors. Taking care of my husband was part of my day, but coping with a crumbling life took most of my time. Our finances were decaying drastically. I became callous when dealing with creditors. Bankruptcy loomed. Should I pray for a large insurance settlement to come my way soon and keep the future from being destroyed or should I pray for my husband's life to continue? Past or future? In the end, I chose to pray for his life. I got the other.

There was no place to find peace. No place of inner quiet to go to. There wasn't time. He and I needed to resolve things. Guilt. One of his prime motivators in life. He needed to understand that I didn't care about guilt. It had nothing to do with life or dying. He was who he was; guilt couldn't change things, could only hasten his dying. It had no place. Anger had fled long ago. Grief would last a long time, but that was a journey to be gotten through, to allow remembrance and integration. He was almost gone, only weeks left, and I was hovering on the verge of a physical collapse. We could accomplish nothing with him back at home and me remaining his only full-time caretaker. The children were becoming increasingly neglected as well. We had to find an alternative. We took him to Hospice House.

Don said that if he went there, he'd never come home again. He was right. But what he had regarded with fear and dread turned out to be a place of release and healing for him. For us all. His family was in attendance, of course. Still hoping. I was able to sleep at night, only listening for the normal sounds of restless children. Our son and daughter found friendship and loving support from the nurses and volunteers.

For the first week of what we had hoped would be a two-week respite, he entertained us. His sense of humor, though somewhat skewed at times, was still intact. He was onstage, the center of attention. He always had an easy way of entertaining people. It kept him from having to deal with the tough stuff. Everyone took a deep breath and heaved a cautious sigh of relief. The second week, he started to release himself, to give up the need to be part of our world. His body responded by letting the disease take hold. He suffered a seizure. His mind became more and more confused. He still recognized people, even old friends who came to visit. But he was also hallucinating and terrified of making a mistake now that would cost his family pain in the future. Panicky late-night phone calls were common. Something that he vaguely remembered doing during the day would become distorted in his mind. He needed to warn me, to have me fix things. To say the least, I never knew what to expect. My thirty-eighth birthday was in the middle of that week. We had a cake and candles for the kids, a few presents. Because our birthdays were ten days apart, for a few days, we were the same age. He never got older.

The last weekend came. It was apparent that we were down to days, perhaps hours. Though his speech was pretty much gone, he was desperate to communicate. He wanted to tell me what he knew. I couldn't understand, but I told him I did, told him it didn't matter. It really didn't. He was sorry. So sorry. "It was OK," I said, "I was going to be OK. The children would be fine. We would always remember. Please don't worry. You've done well" "I'm afraid," he said. "I know you're afraid, but I'm on this side holding your hand. Others are waiting on the other side to take you. You can go."

Two days later, he chose the time. I was home when I knew, just knew, I had to go. It didn't feel urgent. Just important. I had gotten into the routine of making a cup of tea as soon as I got to Hospice House; it gave me a prop, something to hold onto. I knew it was OK to do that now. His dad was on the phone at the nurses' desk, calling from Eugene. I stopped to talk to him for a minute. He asked to talk to Don's sister, who was in his room. I took my tea and went into the room. The time was closer than I was prepared for. He had waited. I had promised to hold his hand. I went to the far side of his bed, took his hand, cried, told him it was OK, they were waiting, and he left.

We had never had a time for him and me just to be at peace together. I felt cheated. There had always been people—family, nurses, friends. A most amazing woman, Jan, the nurse who was attending his death, had sensed this during our time at Hospice. After his sister left the room to call family, Jan closed the door, held me while I cried, and then suggested that I bathe him. A ritual? because his skin had been so sensitized by some aspect of the disease, touching had been torture for him for many months. Now, in peace, I was able to renew that sense of knowing him that was memorized by my hands. To feel one last time that physical being with whom I had shared so much. Eighteen years of growing up together, good and bad, a bicycling vacation in Ireland, children, lots of laughs, lots of anger and hurts, triumphs, griefs, and bitter disappointments. This was something only I could do. A final sharing just for me, for us. I had sent him on his way and now, this last time I was caring for what he had left behind. It was healing slowly emerging from the starting block. I knew there would be blasts of pain yet to come, but in those few private moments, I felt resignation, release, relief. I experienced tears, laughter, awe, calm. And love.

Jan and I dressed him in his Ireland sweatshirt and placed the passage quilt over him. The rest of his family would be coming; it would be a long night. But Don and I had finally had our time together, and I knew that now I could go on and deal with this different life. I also knew that he was already swapping jokes with his Irish ancestors in some peaceful, green version of heaven.

We'll catch up on everything someday.

Taking your time is essential on this journey. It takes time to absorb what has happened. It takes time to be present with your pain. There is no changing the tremendous impact a loved one's death makes. No amount of preparation will take away the pain of the loss. However, the memory of the event becomes the tool to move you through your pain.

Creating Ritual Space

A hospice nurse shared with us the story of a grandfather's preparation for his death. The family, under his guidance, built the coffin he would be buried in. It was built from the trees on the farm that was his home. His wife, sons, daughters, daughters-in-law, grandchild, and friends were part of this building ritual. His wife made the afghan that lined the inside of the coffin. He was comforted and enriched by sharing these moments with his family. A sweetness in the final months of his life became possible; joy was brought to the dying process. It was this bittersweet joy that remained in their memories.

In *The Art of Ritual,* Renee Beck and Sydney Merrick provide a framework for creating meaningful ritual space. The process is described in three stages: the preparation/creation of the ritual, the manifestation, and the grounding and completion. We will take an example of a ritual often offered at Hospice House—the toasting of a person's life at the time of death—to illustrate the progression of these stages.

To prepare, the gathering must identify intentions clearly. The toast is to serve the purpose of helping focus on moments shared with the person who has died. Either wine or juice is poured into crystal glasses. Each person who chooses to be present is given a glass. The next step is the manifestation of the ritual itself. A circle is formed, and the process is explained. Those present are given permission to use this time in any way they choose, although they were explicitly invited to share a memory of the one who has died. In sharing these memories, people create new ones to depart with. The memory may be a story or an account of how the person touched a life, or it may be a prayer (silent or spoken). When it is clear people are through, the ritual moves into its final stage: grounding and closure.

This stage simply involves supporting each other's grief, allowing expression of feelings that have surfaced. It also involves identifying the next step you must walk. The ritual has allowed realization that a death has occurred. Sharing this time with others is a valuable way to release your pain, though it will not take the pain away. The pain will be a common experience for all in the room. Sharing emotional pain has a direct effect on how you will feel. Hearts bursting with sorrow or anger can be eased. The process is like emptying an overflowing cup. Your pain is not taken away; it simply becomes more bearable.

Following the death of their young child Alexandra, her parents Cliff and Regina performed a series of rituals. They bathed her body and dressed her in her favorite pajamas and ruffled socks. They then placed each of her beloved animals inside her favorite blanket. Then they poured the remainder of a special Bach Flower remedy they had given to her during her dying time.

At her funeral they performed the following ritual using the healing power of light. The following is an excerpt from Alexandra Rathburn-Ellis's funeral brochure.

Cliff and Regina Ellis:
 Candles for Alexandra. . . . As we light these five candles, one for each year of your life, they are in

157

honor of you, Alexandra. We light one for grief, one for courage, one for your memory, one for love, and one for healing.

We light this first candle for our grief. Like the heat of this flame, the pain of losing you is so intense. The flame represents the depth of our pain and of our love for you.

The second candle represents courage and strength: what it has taken for you and for us to fight this battle with cancer over the last two years.

This light is in your memory . . . for our family's silliness and laughter, for the times we held and rocked you, the secrets we shared, the songs we sang, the seeds we planted, the funny things you did, and for those looks you gave us with your big blue eyes that told us just what you thought without any words.

The fourth light is the light of love. Day by day we cherish the special place in our hearts that will always be reserved for you. We thank you, Alex . . . the caring, sense of wonder and lesson of acceptance your living has brought to each of us is a lifelong gift.

We light this final candle for healing. Your death has left a space now: in our hearts, our home, our lives. You taught us how to heal . . . through your illness and through your courage during the miracle of your death. Now this is our challenge: to comfort each other, to rebuild our lives, to use the lessons we learned in your struggle with cancer, and to live better lives because of you.

We will always love you, our sweet Alexandra, and we will always miss you.

Sandra Ingerman in her book *Welcome Home* describes ritual as a way to create change. "In order to use ritual, one's body, mind, and spirit must get involved. The mind develops the ritual, the body actually performs it, and the spirit acts as a guide and witness at the ritual." The experience of ritual is unique for each person. Create your own story, your own memories. For the healing power comes from the creative force within you. Miriam tells the story of one man who created a unique, passionate way to give voice to his grief.

Miriam:

I have learned much from those people who allow their grief to be released among other people. These times often occur during middle-of-the-night death visits to homes. One such night comes into my mind. It was summer, the day had been warm, and windows and doors were left open to welcome the wind. As I walked up to the door, I heard the sounds of someone playing old-time gospel music on a hand organ. I stood and listened. The melody was slow and powerful. I realized I had been listening for a few minutes and finally knocked on the door.

The family received me gratefully. There were two daughters who described all that had transpired the past few hours until their mother had died peacefully. This woman's husband stayed in the background, never uttering a word.

I went about my usual ritual—listening to the family, making the necessary calls, cleansing and preparing her body to be received by the funeral home representatives. They arrived. The two daughters spent additional time with them. The husband at one point got up and went to get his hand organ. He proceeded to play passionately. It was the first and only time I have ever seen the funeral home attendants stop, sit down, and take time to listen.

After a few minutes, they took her body and placed it carefully and gently on the stretcher. The sounds coming from the hand organ intensified. It seemed like this man was crying his heart out through this instrument. He played as he walked beside the stretcher. He played as she was placed into the van. He played until the van was out of sight.

I knew it was time for me to leave when the music stopped. It was time for us all to be alone in the silence of the night.

Ritual in the Dying Moment

Ritual may also be present at the time of death. It may be the time many fail to know what to do, overtaken by fear of doing the wrong thing. Our friend Father Bruce Cwiekowski has kindly agreed to share his experience with the dying. His ministry to those dying from AIDS complications has provided him with a remarkable insight. We thankfully pass on his memories.

Father Bruce:
Two aspects of life that are consistent for all of us and yet will differ tremendously is our act of dying and our actual death. There is much mystery that surrounds the process of dying, but as caregivers, we can ease the process and help give birth and life to those for whom we care.

One of the mysteries that surrounds the dying process is that few people are comfortable with the process, and feelings of helplessness can cripple family members and friends that surround the dying person. Death is a natural part of life. We can make the dying time a time of warmth, love, and comfort. We need to be able to trust our inner feelings and do what our heart tells us.

During a recent visit, friends were gathered around a young man not far from his final breath. After some shared prayer time, the friends weren't sure what else they could do for their dying friend. I encouraged them to do what felt natural. One woman asked if it would be all right to get into his bed and hold him. I assured her Mark would not break. Yes, this was a wonderful thing to do.

Slowly, the other friends asked for suggestions. They were told to speak softly and tenderly to Mark. They gathered around the bed, held his hands, spoke their love, their desire that he let go, and their good-byes. Mark died shortly after, but his passing became a peace-filled moment. Grief is never easy, but to watch a loved one die surrounded with this much love and devotion supports those left behind and makes death more peaceful.

In another instance, a young man was dying, and his partner was looking for support. After spending time with the dying man, I was able to spend time with his partner. We talked of ways that he could ease Adam through the dying process. Several days later, I was able to talk with the partner about Adam's recent death. The partner told me how he took two champagne glasses and placed candles in them. He also cut three rosebuds and placed them around the candles. All the while he was doing his tasks, he explained to Adam what he was doing. Finally, he took Adam's hand and began to pray the Our Father. Before the

prayer was finished, Adam died. The partner kept re-
peating to me, "How beautiful his death was. I never
realized that death could be so beautiful."

Ritual plays an important role in this process, both
for the one who is dying and the loved ones who are
gathered around. In another example, I was asked to
visit with a family that had been shunned by its church.
The mother, who was the primary caregiver, spoke of
reading the Bible daily and was confused about one section. After she read it to me, I explained that this was a
ritual celebrated in the church for those who were sick.
She asked if we could do something similar for her son.
Together, we prayed, blessed oil, and anointed her
dying son. I told her that she should keep the oil, and
each night as they prayed together, she should once
again anoint her child.

In times of great emotional distress, we need to
do what feels right, to follow our hearts and fill the
room with warmth and love, to help make the dying
process a moment of grace. Soft music, candles or soft
glowing light, physical contact, gentle and loving
words, tears, the opportunity to speak our good-byes,
all make the process real and hope filled. Dying and
death do not have to be grim experiences. The sadness
will be there, but by following our hearts, death becomes new life.

Most hospices have a pastoral care coordinator or
counselor who is available to assist the dying one's family
and the staff to make and heal from the death of a loved
one. Often, this involves improvising a ritual to comfort
and commemorate. In the words of Richard Groves, director of pastoral care at Hospice of Bend, Oregon, this is a
way to culminate our search for a meaningful path from

endings to new beginnings. Here, he shares his guidelines for designing rituals:

1. Listen to people's stories.
2. Know their needs and heritage.
3. Consider your role in the dialogue.
4. Pay attention to the space and the appropriate symbols.
5. Consider the wisdom of the ages.
6. Design a shared witness, that is, a ceremony that includes everyone.

Whatever you choose to do for closure following a death, keep it simple. Allow yourself to be creative. Honor the one who has died, and honor your own grief and sadness. The chart on the next page provides suggestions for rituals. The list is by no means complete. It suggests some possibilities and options, and we hope you find it useful.

RITUALS FOR REMEMBERING

Ritual	*Symbolism*
Light candle near the bed.	Candles symbolize illumination and clarity. Choose one that is special to you or to the one who has died.
Place a passage quilt on the one who has died.	Place a favorite blanket or quilt over the person's body. It can be buried with the body or removed prior to the burial. This is a symbol of completion.
Toast the one who has died.	Give a glass to each person. Form a circle around the bed. The toast can be shared aloud or made silently. The drink is a symbol of new life.
Bathe and prepare the body.	This is a sacred moment of ritual. The body is bathed, and perhaps holy oils are applied. The ritual symbolizes cleansing and new life and invites a final moment of physical connection with the person.
Place a flower on the bed after the body has been removed.	A favorite flower is placed on the bed. It is also a symbol of new life.
Family and friends create quilt squares.	Use a square of material and fabric pens. Write your message. Decorate with images that reflect your thoughts and feelings about your relationship with the one who has died; use the images to express anything left unsaid. This process can be a step toward completion.

7

Death As a Healing Experience

Our final chapter is a collection of stories that people close to us have written about their support of others through the dying experience. Each story can be seen as a culmination of the midwife's role in honoring and appreciating those who have been lovingly cared for. These accounts also help show how an atmosphere of hope, faith, and love can transform the death experience and bring a sense of peace and joy to the final moment.

Throughout much of this book, we have discussed what death is not: it is not bad or a failure, nor is it necessarily a tragedy or even the end. In a sense, what we have done in this chapter is ask our friends to tell us their stories about what death *is*, as much as this is possible. We who work with the dying can often struggle with the words to describe death. Our culture expects to hear only about the negative side of dying—the sorrow, the pain, the exhaustion—and may flinch when we point to the bright side—the healing, the joy, the laughter. Perhaps Walt Whitman was thinking of this when he wrote:

> Has anyone supposed it lucky to be born?
> I hasten to inform him or her, it is just as lucky to die, and I know it.
> I pass death with the dying, and birth with the new-washed babe
> ... and am not contained between my hat and boots.
>
> —WALT WHITMAN, *Leaves of Grass*

Although we, unlike Walt Whitman, have never used the word *lucky* to describe death, we do try to make the point that death can be a healing, positive, natural experience. Yet, we can be seen as minimizing the difficulty of dying when we use these words. For this reason, we have chosen to include stories that encompass the totality of what death is, both good and bad. We have found that when the story of death is told by someone who has walked the path, the effect is profound. These stories are more than just the sum of their words. They took great courage to write, and the very action of writing released and healed painful layers of grief. These stories are small pieces of peoples' souls.

You may find that this chapter is difficult at times to read, and it is probably not a good idea to read it all in one sitting. Sometimes, another's words may evoke feelings that had remained unconscious; the sudden awareness of these buried emotions can be painful and healing at the same time. Be sure to seek support through this process. Take the time to let the wisdom of each storyteller's words seep in, and don't rush yourself.

Healing and Suffering

To refer to death as a healing journey does not mean that there is no darkness or pain. Quite the contrary. If we walk honestly through any of the dark times in our lives, there will be sorrow. It is the belief of many that darkness and light are part of the same reality. The yin and the yang, the theory of opposites attracting, daylight moving to darkness, all reinforce this belief.

Ram Dass is an author and workshop leader who works with dying people. He explained suffering in one of his workshops in this way:

> When you look at the world you see suffering everywhere . . . if you are going to be able to see someone else's beauty, you need to be able to acknowledge your own beauty. In a similar way if you are going to be available for someone else's suffering, you have to be able to acknowledge your own suffering and be able to understand the nature of suffering in such a way that you have converted the quality of suffering in yourself . . . suffering brings you closer to the great mystery. You don't invite suffering into your life but when it comes you work with the opportunity of transformation. It is a gift given allowing you to come home.

When we speak of dying here, it is as an event to be acknowledged as an acceptable reality. This revelation may not come all at once (or ever) for everyone. It may exist in pieces, as a puzzle that requires years to put together. This is another reason we present other people's memories. Our own memories are limited. This adds to the mystery of death. We do not pretend to understand it in completion. Perhaps this book will provide some additional pieces in your puzzle as it has for us.

An experience of Miriam's points to the way in which our hearts can sometimes open slowly to the reality of death. Her intellectual understanding of death came quickly; as a nursing student this knowledge was imparted through study and training. It took another two years to perceive an understanding within her heart.

Miriam:

My time spent nursing at Hospice House finally led me to an opening of my heart. I can remember the moment. My dear friend Bea and I went to a movie that portrayed the journey of two women who had been best friends since childhood. One friend ultimately died. The other cared for her until the last breath and beyond by becoming the mother of the child her friend had left behind.

I was crying at the end of the movie and still crying forty-five minutes later. Through my tears, I was seeing all those whose deaths I had attended. It was like a stream of faces and memories racing before my eyes. My tears were a flood washing over me. It was the most cleansing of experiences. I had up to that point never shed a tear of good-bye for those who had died. I am not exactly certain what led me to this moment of truth.

I only know that I had by then experienced many deaths without an intentional letting go. I had rigidly held all those powerful memories inside myself until they burst forth, like water flowing from a damn when the gates are opened. I realized my heart was finally opening to understanding and accepting this mystery of death. The tears come much more easily and abundantly now. I realize how important release is, not only for the dying ones, but for those who care for them.

There is a great controversy here in Oregon regarding a patient's right to die through assisted suicide. The basic question that a person making such a decision must ask is, Have I made an informed choice? In our view, an informed choice means a decision has been made with the heart, mind, and spirit. It is not enough to receive factual and technical input. Our heart and soul must also be involved to allow reflection and understanding. This informed choice must therefore come from a place of love, not fear. Helen Schucman's *Course in Miracles* describes the existence of only two emotions: fear and love. A decision reflecting an understanding with our heart, mind, and spirit should bring a greater sense of peace and resolve. For most, the ability to make such an informed decision takes an investment of time and energy.

In many ways the issue of assisted suicide has brought death to the forefront of our public conscience. Finally, we are naming our fears and concerns about this life process. This book for us is a way to respond to those concerns. We are offering another approach to the dying journey. The stories were written about people who chose a natural death. Their words tell of the difficulties of their choices. They also speak of the joy and healing that comes only when we sit in the darkness. They tell of their journey as they walk toward the light.

It is not our intention to romanticize or in any way underestimate the tall mountain each of these dying people and their loved ones have to climb. It is our intention to throw a lifeline to each of them, to offer hope in the midst of sorrow, to offer updated information and resources. No matter what choice you make regarding your death moment, may you find peace and support and hope in your journey.

Jan:

Ruth died on Easter Sunday after a courageous fight against breast cancer. Three years later, I find my heart still has tender places when I think of her. I miss her hugs and her laughter. I miss her rigorous honesty when I would ask her a question. I miss her quiet presence in my dark moments. Her dying time taught me a great deal about how hard it is when we have expectations about the way things should be rather than how they are. For me, this was the hardest part to heal after her death.

When Ruth decided it was time for hospice care, my own letting go process began. How do you say good-bye to a dear friend? How do you say good-bye to the long chats over a cup of tea? Or the rituals you have created over the years that celebrate life's ups and downs? I was not ready to say good-bye to my healer friend who was a partner in therapeutic touch.

I needed an outlet for my sorrow. I found solace in living in the moment. Or hearing her weak, gentle voice tell me how beautiful the winter's first snowfall was. I savored the quiet times of sitting together, watching her crochet her unborn grandson's first blanket. I cherished laying next to her as our friend Nan sang the song "Across the River" to us. Each moment was another letting go. Each moment brought me closer to the realization that our friendship would be growing in ways we had not predicted. My earth angel friend was traveling ahead of me to the places we had dreamed about together.

Music has always provided a healing energy for

me. When Ruth was dying, I wrote her a song. In the
time that has passed since her death, I realize that I
wrote the song for me—for my grief. To this day, this
song carries me through the waves of sadness and
missing my dear old friend.

FOR RUTH
I'm gonna miss you my old friend
This lifetime is coming to an end
Our love has taken seasons to grow
Now winter has come
Oh I feel so afraid of the cold.

My old friend, I know I'll see you again
But the chill is moving in and springtime
seems so far away

My old friend
I want to cradle you in my arms
Wipe the sorrow from your eyes
But I know you must journey
out of the darkness all alone

My old friend
when my heartbeat sings her last song
it's you who'll be waiting to take me home
You'll ask me where I've been
and why I took so long
And I'll say

My old friend
its good to see you again
we'll laugh till the early dawn
you'll cradle me in your arms as I sing

THE TRUE WORK OF DYING

I've missed the fire in your eyes
and the sparkle of your smile
as we'd talk away the hours
My old friend

It's good to see you again
Ruth, my old friend
It's good to have you back again.

I remember people saying to me after Ruth died how lucky I was to have such a powerful angel in heaven. I remember saying, "Oh, but I want her here, not there." I have had to learn and adjust to our new way of relating. Ruth visits me in the sacred sweat lodges she loved so much. On my journeys, she stands strong and present as my spirit guide. In my dark moments, she will tenderly place unseen arms around me and rock me lovingly until the light is once again visible.

Ruth has taught me about patience. That there is no right length of time to grieve. To be prepared for the unexpected moments when tears will flow from deep within me. When the tears flow, she taught me never to hand a tissue to the one who is crying because that tells him or her to stop. She taught me to love the earth in all its glory.

More than anything, Ruth and her family taught me the sacredness of a natural death. Her death was a long, hard labor. There was much sorrow and loss surrounding her transition. Yet, in the midst of all of the darkness, Ruth would see a light in the east that represented transformation. As she was wrapped safely in the angel blanket that others before had used, she healed herself and each of us who were with her. The members of her family welcomed me into their intimate deathing time and shared their wife, mother, sister, and friend with me. For those sacred moments, I am eternally grateful.

The following story reveals another person's time of revelation. It speaks to the time and energy required for them to leave this earth in peace.

Father Bruce:

Several weeks ago, I received a phone call from a local hospice, informing me that a client was requesting to see a priest. The young man had been informed that day he had less than two months to live and he wished to make peace with his God.

At our first meeting, he informed me that prayer had always been an important part of his life. With his illness progressing, he requested a crucifix to hang on his wall and a medal of Jesus to wear around his neck. I assured him that his request would be fulfilled and offered him the opportunity to receive the sacraments. He stared at me for a minute and then broke into tears. He told me that he had been away from church for twenty-five years and never felt worthy of receiving Holy Communion. His greatest desire was to be able to receive communion again.

As we celebrated the Sacrament of Reconciliation, he cried. As I anointed him with oil and offered him the gift of the Eucharist, the tears continued. There were tears of pain and sadness, but also tears of life and joy. After that, John's eyes sparkled each time I visited and brought him the gift of the Eucharist.

One evening, I was called and told John was in

the active phase of dying and requested to see me. By the time I reached him, he was barely conscious, with shallow breathing. I told him I was there and offered to pray with him. After reciting some of his favorite prayers, John's breathing became less pronounced. I told him that I loved him and that God loved him and was waiting for him. At that moment, John's eyes sparkled one more time and he breathed his last.

Often, I have been aware of God's presence at the time of death, and John's death was no exception. It was a sacramental moment in my life. The God who gives each of us life was there to welcome John into eternal life. John's simplicity and sincerity have touched many people. May he continue to pray for us now and at the hour of our death.

There is also an enrichment for our heart and spirit in sharing the memories of those who experience the dawning of death's approach. A home health nurse shared the following story with us about the importance of quiet presence.

Sherry LiaBraaten:
In my hospice nursing work, I once cared for a woman in her final stages of gastric cancer. Word among the home health nurses was that she was very angry in the present stage of her disease, refusing all care except for dressing changes of her catheter site. In addition, she refused to have the nursing staff in her room (except for that procedure). So we positioned ourselves right outside her door at the family's request to observe and monitor her needs.

After having been off for a few days, I returned to

her home, reading numerous nursing notations regarding "hallucinations" and "unusual, busy motions" with her upper extremities. Late that evening,
I, too, watched as she began busily moving her arms
about, turning her head side to side as she responded
in German to questions and directions coming from
elsewhere. All the while, she had her eyes closed, and
the angry frown that she'd worn since I met her had
vanished.

Her sister, ready to leave for home, joined me in
the doorway. We watched her together for only a few
minutes before her sister, who was at first frightened,
exclaimed that she was speaking to their father, who
had died many years before. We continued to watch
together for nearly an hour and realized that she was
washing and drying dishes and putting them away.
With the motions corresponding to exact cupboard lo-
cations, she carefully replaced each dish and glass. I
discovered that she'd been an avid cook and enter-
tainer, taking great pleasure in having friends over
for dinner.

As her activity began to slow and the dishes were
done, her sister translated for me, "Papa, I'll be there
soon, I'm almost done." She died that night, an hour
after I left.

No hallucinations, just the last bit of work to finish up.

This song was written by Dr. Patti Meyer for her
friend Jane on the one-year anniversary of her death. Her
mother was still so grief stricken that it provided a way
to tell the mom that her daughter had been not forgotten
and still lived on in our hearts.

THE TRUE WORK OF DYING

YOU'RE AN ANGEL NOW
We were only children when you first became my friend
Playing in the summer sun, running with the wind
From dawn to dusk, games of make-believe
We laughed the days away
We never knew the love we shared
Grew stronger day by day

You're an angel now, in the heavens up above
You walk with God and sing your songs
And send this world your love
For I see you in the summer sun, I feel you in the wind
But my heart still longs to see you smile
And hear your laugh again

As we grew into our teens, we became as One
Sharing all our joys and dreams, talking until dawn
I watched you grow, I learned to love
As you reached out to me
I never realized, friend, that our time would soon be
    ending

You're an angel now, in the heavens up above
You walk with God, and sing your songs
And send this world your love
For I see you in the summer sun, I feel you in the wind
But my heart still longs to see you smile
And hear your laugh again

We were in the prime of life when it came to be
God was calling you, my friend, "Come and be with me"
In the spring, your days grew short
Your Love-Light still shone bright

DEATH AS A HEALING EXPERIENCE

Your spirit lives within us all, who shared with you
    this life

For I see you in the summer sun, I feel you in the wind
I know you in the star-lit sky
Then hear your laugh again

You're an angel now in the heavens up above
You walk with God and sing your songs
And send this world your love
For I see you in the summer sun, I feel you in the wind
I know you in the star-lit sky
Then hear your laugh again

You're an angel now
Send this world your love
You're an angel now

One of the many blessings of working in hospice are
the many ways families and loved ones experience and
acknowledge their dying one. At Hospice House, we had
a blank book at the end of the hall in which patients,
nurses, staff, and family would write whatever was in
their hearts. Within its pages were previously untold stories of pain and the healing that comes from the experience of death and dying. It had the ability to hold
emotions that no human could hold her- or himself.

A father wrote this story in the healing book at Hospice House following his son's death. Shawn had found
the butterfly to be a powerful spirit guide as he journeyed
toward death. Friends and family know now that when a
butterfly lights beside you, Shawn has come by to lighten
your load.

THE TRUE WORK OF DYING

Rich:

My Dear Son Shawn,

Happy Easter, Son. Through your strength and courage, you have given your family a rebirth, an opportunity to grow in love and compassion and to strengthen the bonds that have always existed. Yes, Son, your life has had a purpose. You were vulnerable, lonely, unsure of what you were doing in this world, and so wonderful. You were given the freedom to be you—I hope this is one of your most valuable treasures. As time has passed, we have looked at this mature young man and discovered a whole new person—like us in some ways, unlike us in others. We have been so blessed because we have found a loving and lifelong friend. In your communion with the loving and caring people of Hospice House, you discovered yourself—the real you, the beautiful you. Now as God speeds you on your journey, fly, my little butterfly, fly.

> A butterfly lights beside us
> like a sunbeam
> And for a brief moment its glory and
> beauty
> belong to our world.
> But then it flies on again,
> and though we wish
> it could have stayed,
> we feel so lucky
> to have seen it.

God love you,
Dad

DEATH AS A HEALING EXPERIENCE

The grace of perseverance is an ever-present reality for those who care for the dying. A friend and nurse shared this story about her mother's dying time. It took great courage and strength for Dolores to put into words what the experience had meant to her. It is this courage that has taught us the words that this book needed to say. The unsung heroes are those who provide loving care to their families and loved ones.

Dolores:

Because Mom was a healthy, robust woman, we had no idea that an illness that showed its face in her fifty-sixth year ever so casually, seeming like the flu, would end up taking her life three battle-scarred years later.

"You have ten days to live if you decide not to seek treatment. We may extend the lifeline to about one year . . . no guarantees."

Mom survived for three years longer than her initial prognosis of ten days. Her treatment, her faith and attitude, her family, physicians, friends, each contributed energy and ability to allow her to continue until her "earth work" was done. There would be intensive care units, pheresis, blood products ("liquid gold" as Mom called it), tubes in many orifices, and fevers. These would be interspersed with trips to Reno, births of more grandchildren, and lots of love and sharing. She loved life and most of its gifts, especially family, friends, and flowers. Her three children were her special joy. She said that parents are like artists, children are their paintings, and hers were her masterpieces.

The end would finally come when there were no more rabbits to pull from the hat. The tried and true chemotherapy agents as well as the experimental ones had been used up. A decision had been made for no life-saving measures.

It was midnight. Her temperature had reached 105. I placed cold washcloths on her body, but they would warm up as fast as I could change them.

"Are you scared, Mom?" I asked. "No, there is nothing to be afraid of" was her reply. By 5:00 A.M. her blood pressure began to fall. Her pulse was racing and her breathing was rapid. Mom's eyes became hazy; it appeared that she was having great difficulty seeing although her sense of hearing was acute.

Mom's oncologist arrived. He had been the magician who had given her hope and love and a sense of pride as he wove a beautiful relationship into the practice of his medicine. He whispered into her ear, "Mary, I have learned a great deal from you." A gentle kiss on the forehead and a loving hug were his farewell.

Mom seemed able to hear but unable to respond. Her rhythmic breathing was labored and intense. Her gaze was unfocused and far away, yet her presence was greater than ever. At 11:55 P.M., her son Gary arrived. Quietly whispering in her ear, his arms enfolded the hot and worn-out body of his mother. I placed her arms around him for a final hug. "I love you, Mom," he said, "and there could never be a more wonderful mother than you." We both joined hands and touched her. As one of her sons prayed aloud the 'Our Father,' asking for the Lord to welcome her into heaven and angels to take her up, Mom breathed one final breath. The moment was literally suspended in time. There was a silence so gripping that its power will last a lifetime in the memory of those who surrounded her. "Breathe, Mom," I urged as I shook her. But there was no breath to follow. Mom's spirit had been lifted.

I had so feared the moment when the final good-bye would come. I was afraid that I would not be able to tear myself away from her body. I had nightmares about hospital staff having to pull me off her body, not being able to let go of her, not being able to say good-bye.

For all of my life, my mom was my sustaining force. One that years before I had become committed to in an unspoken agreement. As the last month of her life approached, I became fearful for my own life, not seeing a future for myself beyond her death. My brother encouraged me to share my fear with Mom. Though it was difficult, I did. That's when she told me about children being like a painter's masterpiece. She told me that her purpose was to provide life, not take it away. She told me that I must go on living the life she had given and worked to provide.

The realization that Mom's time on earth was limited came slowly for me. I believe that she held on until she felt that I was able to let go. As for my nightmares about being able to let go of her body, a strange thing happened. When Mom took her last breath, it was truly a sacred moment. There is a fine line between life and death. As her spirit went up, it became obvious to me that her body was just a worn-out "suit of clothes" I had served her well, and I felt the body should be respected, but the mother that I knew and loved was not there. Her spirit was not in her body. It was not hard to part with "worn-out clothes" because I knew and felt a different presence. It was not her body I was in love with, it was her spirit.

As a nurse working in the emergency department, I've seen death come in all forms. Much too quickly for some, no time for preparation, no time for good-byes. For others, the road to death is long, the time for good-byes is long, but the suffering and struggle are a large price to pay.

It has been nine years since my mother's death. As I write this piece, I am physically ill to my stomach. It doesn't get easier with time, it gets different. The memories and unraveling of a relationship and grief unfold with time. For me, therapy and a gifted therapist have been a tremendous help. It takes years of formation for us to develop, and depending on our experiences, it takes years for us to understand our development and integrate our losses. My mother's death was my greatest pain and in an odd way my greatest blessing. I have learned lessons about life and relationships that could not be taught by any other experience. I still waiver and at times falter on the path of healing. But never would I trade my precious memories, my experiences with my mother, or my newfound knowledge of independent life. The task now at hand is to live out the masterpiece . . .

It has been a gift to us to have worked with so many wonderful people in hospice. These men and women who devote much of their time and hearts to caring for others are inspiring not only to the dying, but to us as well. Miriam has had the privilege of working with the author of the next account since 1990. He shares in his poem the struggle and truth of so many who have died of AIDS.

WHAT WILL BE TOMORROW?

Last week my son married
today, my brother comes home to die.
The front door opens.
The AIDS comes in and drags him along.
His yellow skin and uninterruptible cough greet us
and point the way to a new family healing
through my mother's nervous stare and
her sterilizing the china by replacing it with Chinette
through my disbelieving chatter at the realization that
a week ago I saw
only my son's wedding and not my brother's 4 sizes
    too small
body lost in a tuxedo suit.
Before he dies, the healing must come or we'll lose him!
His cough continues, our decisions are made without
    conferring.
We steady his walk to what is now my mother's bed
It had been our parents' bed before dad died
and was ours when each was born at home.
He leads us, I throw back the sheet, my mother
pulls down the family quilt hoping its history will
    ease
his uncontrollable shivering on this 90 degree day.
Quiet, my brother, know, at last, our fears of this dis-
    ease have died
you are my brother, her son, the disease
tried to change that and failed!
In this summer heat, on this summer day,
we pull the blankets up to our chins, we hold and
    rock him,

we experience his growing quiet as my brother, her
    son, dies.
My mother and I lie motionless, holding him.
The death peels back my soul, my mother sobs.
The summer sun melts into an orange glow.

                —TIM ZOEBELIEN, *Life Poems*

The poem brings out three themes involved in the
process of dying. The first relates to the isolation that can
sometimes occur. When a person is dying, those connected with that person confront the impending loss, past
losses, and their own mortality. Some friends and family
distance themselves from their feelings and the dying person; some come closer. This highlights how the dying process encompasses many other losses (loss of friendship,
memory losses, loss of dreams) besides the impending
death. The fear created by the misunderstanding of AIDS
can cause the isolation to be even more profound when
family, friends, and the community ostracize the dying
one and stay away.

The second theme is the struggle to adjust to changes
and to honor relationships. This poem focuses on the
family putting aside their fear and honoring their relationship with its son/brother. We see this occur repeatedly if people don't simply run away. Both subtle and
profound healing can occur.

The third theme highlights the immediacy, intensity,
and sadness you feel when someone you love dies. Death
will eventually arrive for everyone, and when it does,
there are no do-overs. That is why it's important not to
run from your inner struggle.

Singer/songwriter Nan Collie wrote a song, "We
Won't Forget," in memory of those who have died from
AIDS:

DEATH AS A HEALING EXPERIENCE

There is a hole in the sky tonight, shining star has
    lost its light
Another brother's gone from sight, a comet in the sky
He feels the night come closing in, who falls next,
    when will it end
shadows on his wall begin to chase him into time

But who is counting as precious lives are lost
This act of loving has carried quite a cost
Don't hide your head, our loving brings us home
Don't hide your tears, no you are not alone we are
    here

Daniel walks down to the store, a cup of coffee noth-
    ing more
his trembling brings it to the floor so all who know
    can see
The sharpened edges, piercing bones, hollow eyes that
    head for home
he picks up the pieces all alone, as others look away

But who is counting as moments pass
a woman reaches and touches fragile glass
she won't hide her head because our loving brings
    us home
She won't hide her heart, she says you are not alone—
    we are here

Steve rises slowly from a tossed and tumbled night
sheets are shrouds and blankets cover ghosts who've
    taken flight
Lovers, dancers, poets, painters, he has touched
    them all

THE TRUE WORK OF DYING

In dreams they are returning, he can hear them call

And he is counting as precious moments pass
yes, he is reaching, for the angels come at last
he won't hide his death, his dying brings him home
now he can rest, no he is not alone
yes, he has blessed the circles he has known
with his last breath another star is born

We won't forget: Keeston, Charles, William, Shawn,
    Ted, Jim, Don, Peter, Chris, Bill, Alexandra

The following story comes from a remarkable group
of brothers and sisters with whom Miriam had the honor
of working. Even this story, which is primarily written
by one of the sisters, has received input and approval by
all of the others. Their ability to communicate in a loving, competent, and mindful way is a tribute to their family life. They are family in the strongest sense of the
word. This story serves for us as a model of what is possible when you enter into this time of dying as a family.

Valerie (on behalf of the Ricker family):
July 1995
    As I write this, our extended family (six children,
three in-laws, and four grandchildren) is gathered for
a week's vacation at the Oregon coast. This vacation,
which was to be a family reunion and summer get-
away, was planned by our mother ten months ago.
Eight months ago we became aware of the metastasis
of her cancer and the likelihood that she would not
be alive for this reunion. Repeatedly through the last
two months of her life, Mom encouraged us to keep
this vacation time, saying that it would be an impor-

tant time for us to reconnect (as our homes span across the United States and Europe) and we could scatter her ashes together.

As I reflect on my mother's life, I realize she started, more than twenty-five years ago, working to break her own, our family's, and her friends' fear of death and dying. Mom's style for facing change or issues she did not understand or feared was to do research on them and learn as much as she could. In this way, she was prepared and could imagine many of the possible outcomes. Also it prompted her to identify what was important to her, so she could think out her choices and share her rationale.

Her work to get our immediate and extended family to talk about illness and death escalated when our father was diagnosed with cancer in 1971. Our parents took stock of what was important in their lives, and as a result, we lived our daily lives more consciously, taking advantage of special opportunities as they arose without postponing them to unknown future dates.

Dad died suddenly. His death was not what Mom had envisioned it would be. There was insufficient time to gather the family and to live his death. I suspect this gave her a greater desire for her own death to be more purposeful.

Mom was diagnosed with uterine cancer two and one-half years prior to her death. Many times during that period, through several surgeries and radiation therapy, she said she was thankful she had cancer rather than cardiac disease. She felt that her death would be more gradual and that she would be able to tie up loose ends and say good-byes. In the fall of 1994, Mom reached the point where her health would

THE TRUE WORK OF DYING

not allow the quality of life she had previously enjoyed. Mom had always stated clearly that the quality of life was more important to her than quantity of life.

In November 1994, Mom set out on the last leg of her earthly journey. She was confined to bed and needed the assistance of others to accomplish many of the physical tasks of daily life. Our family and Mom's health care team were aware of her desire to remain in her own home. Hospice was invited in, and Mom began the work of actively living her death. This is when she did the bulk of her teaching, while making the process a positive and comfortable one for others. Our mother lived her death and broke the stereotype of death being a sad and negative process that should be avoided at all costs. Mom was always open about her life and therefore was the same about her death. If you were physically present, she gently brought you into the process often before you had a chance to think about running away.

To us, our family and her many friends, Mom was a very special and unique person. One part of her life that we would like to share is how she involved her family and friends in living her dying and death. She brought together several people who had been important at separate, distinct periods in her life and created a new community, united in the mission of living her death.

During her final month of life, Mom had requested that we read to her from May Sarton's book, *A Reckoning*. The main character speaks of life being like a spider web; in order to die, one needs to cut the individual lines of that web. Mom had read this book nearly fifteen years ago and said she still held onto the book because she "thought she might need it sometime in the future." Looking back, I think this provided a framework for how she wanted her own dying process to occur.

The last eight to ten weeks of Mom's life was the process of cutting those individual lines of the web of her life. It started out with a large support group of family and friends coming to take a turn at being her caretaker and saying their formal and informal good-byes. The community, love, and togetherness were important to her, the dying person, and to us, her family. We believe that for Mom, nonfamily community involvement was important for two reasons: (1) their physical assistance as well as other gestures of support eased her feelings of being burdensome to her children and (2) it assisted her in disengaging from our family. It gave her a few "outsiders" to whom she felt close, yet with whom she did not have to be strong. Though she was open and forthright with the family, there were some things she, as a parent, found difficult to say to her children.

My three brothers, two sisters, and I visited Mom at different points during the Thanksgiving holidays and each of us received his or her initial training in caregiving. With the help of Mom's friends, we worked out a staggered schedule of caregiving. My brother John was to fill an eight-day gap just prior to Christmas. His story illuminates how Mom led and supported us as we did what we thought might be impossible to do for our parent, especially a son for his mother.

As that time approached, both Mom and John had concerns about how it would work out. They both felt uneasy about the level of bodily/physical intimacy that would be required. John recalled a friend's remark at a time when the friend was caring for his mother that helped John overcome his uneasiness. The friend had said, "I don't find it easy to help her on the toilet, but I figure she did this for me when I was not able to do it for myself. I want to be able to do that for her now, when she can no longer do these things."

During the three weeks John was in the United States, he discovered new sides to Mom. It was perhaps due to the fact that he ran the household and therefore came into contact with and got to know her friends from a different vantage point than in his prior visits. He saw what a great person she was through her friends' eyes and experienced this to a small extent himself. He felt it was a bittersweet experience as it also revealed to him the special bond between mother and child, a much more complicated relationship. The bitter part was seeing her interaction with friends and realizing that he had never known her in the same way; the sweetness was that he had this glimpse of his mother's uniqueness and recognized it.

John is grateful that he and Mom overcame their initial qualms so that he could play a role in caregiving for her. This role, especially the eight days he did it on his own, was a very important element for him in the process of letting go of her. As the day for his departure approached, he realized all the more that the hardest thing he would have to say to her was that she had his blessing to go. It was true even if his heart was still saying, "Please stay." Through the morning of his departure, he still hoped that she would live through the spring, that he would be able to visit her one more time. He realized, however, that should that happen he would then want to bargain for yet another three months and after that another three and so on. At some point he would have to accept her approaching death and let go and that to help her it needed to happen before he left for Europe.

As her energy diminished, the circle of people Mom allowed to support her directly was reduced to immediate family and select friends. Mom identified specific activities these people could do to assist her in tying up her loose ends. An example of her assisting others in her dying occurred with her best friend. Mom was aware of her friend's discomfort with her impending death and that because of this she had not been visiting Mom. Mom said that we needed to find a way to bring her friend into her daily life and her care circle. She decided that her friend should be the one to feed her lunch each day, that this would give her friend a responsibility and would draw her back into Mom's inner circle. Despite Mom's diminished energy, her trademark openness, grace, and humor shone throughout this process.

Since Mom's death, there has been a universal theme running through the comments of all who were with her in her final months. All have felt that their experience with her had been a gift. Many commented that they no longer viewed death in a fearful way. Rather, their eyes had been opened to how it could be done. Many say they now feel at peace with her death because they were able to experience her dying and know she died in the manner she wanted. None of this could have happened

1. If Mom had not been mindful of the eventuality of death and had not verbalized her desires.

2. If she and our father had not been respectful and intentional in their parenting, so that my siblings and I were able to work together to make her last wishes a reality.

3. Without the support of Mom's and our individual support communities (systems).

4. Without the support and guidance of hospice.

The hospice team members who were involved in Mom's care were unique angels. We are particularly appreciative of Miriam and her journeying with us in the last three days of Mom's life. Miriam gave words and definitions to the changes we saw in Mom's physical and at times mental status. She walked us through the possible changes that might occur as Mom approached death and what her dying might be like. This assured us of the process and enabled us to be calm and to experience her death without outside intervention.

The early version of this book, which Miriam gave us the last week of Mom's death, was most helpful to us and our mother. Different people read the entirety to Mom. Even though at times we thought Mom was asleep, she was listening to it all. This book in particular helped her to let go of her body and helped us children and friends to allow her to go soar with the angels. The analogy with the birthing process helped us to understand and accept the process of assisting Mom's spirit in leaving this physical plane and moving on. It enabled a peace and naturalness to surround us and comforted Mom that all was happening as it should. She was surrounded by love and loved ones at all times in her journey. She was a courageous and open teacher to the end. Those of us remaining felt most honored to have been a part of her dying as she had bestowed upon us her last gift.

A brother, sister, and I were present when Mom died. The preparations Mom had made to make sure we knew how things should proceed in the immediate hours after her death gave us peace and calm. Mom's body remained in her home for more than six hours after her death. We had an informal wake of family and those friends who had been included in the last stage of her dying. Her minister led us in an anointing ceremony that celebrated the life she led and the body that had hosted her spirit.

Though we miss her, we relish the thought that she has been reunited with our father and that they once again accompany each other on the next part of their eternal journey. Mom viewed death as "the doorway to another level of understanding in God's perfect plan." So God's speed to you, our amazing treasure!

Our friend Evelyn wrote this account for us to share on a local radio show. Her story points to the spiritual gifts that are given to many during the time of dying. We, the readers, benefit from Evelyn's courage.

Evelyn:

It was early morning on Holy Saturday [the day before Easter]. My sister Kay ("Katie") had been receiving care at home as she was dying from cancer. Her primary caretaker, Catherine Ann, had been in bed sleeping for some hours. Kay had asked Theresa and me, two of her sisters, to be with her until her death was over. We had spent many nights sitting next to her bed.

We had a candle burning in her room that was to

remain until Kay took her last breath. We knew this was fast approaching as her breathing had become very raspy on Good Friday evening. Hospice had given us a patch to place on her ear that would help with the fluid buildup and make it easier for Kay to breathe.

My eyes were closed as I gently rubbed Kay's hand. I opened them up to see a shadow on the window of her room. It was as if snow were falling around a beautiful woman. I felt this woman to be the Virgin Mary. My heart felt peaceful and I was awestruck. As the shadow left, the room filled with light. My other sister, Theresa, said she had been almost irritated with the flickering of the candle, but at this moment, it began to burn very brightly. It was as if someone had turned on a light in the room.

I had wanted to hold my sister in my arms for several days but did not because I knew it would hurt her. Now, it seemed like the time would be right. As quickly as I thought it, I heard a very clear voice saying, "Do not touch her. She belongs to me." I moved back and felt a power that I cannot express. Kay now drew a short breath, then quit. I touched my sister Theresa's arm and said, "It's over." Theresa said, "No!" and Kay drew three more quiet breaths, and it was done.

The hours following were filled with her family and celebration. We touched her body, as we felt her free of it. Her daughters placed flowers in her hair. During this process, a gentle, magical smile appeared on her face. It was truly a celebration of love. We stayed with her until everyone had come in to say good-bye and we could feel her spirit leave. It was over and her joy had begun.

DEATH AS A HEALING EXPERIENCE

The following story was written by a mother about her nine-year-old son, who died from brain cancer. This young man was part of a community that was transformed by his short life. During the course of his illness and treatment, many prayed for him. In fact, the local Roman Catholic community kept open a chapel in memory of Robby for eucharistic adoration according to its tradition. This means that during a designated twenty-four-hour period at least one person was always present in the chapel praying before a *consecrated host* (i.e., the body of Christ), which is held in a vessel called a *monstrance*.

The transcendence of this faithful community continued after Robby died. The community now has perpetual eucharistic adoration in the same chapel all day, every day, due in no small part due to those who participated in the prayer vigil for Robby. The benefit of prayer brought peace to this believing community even while it had to say good-bye and let go of that precious child. This was only possible because the community knew Robby would be received in heaven.

Janie:
Faith is the realization of what is hoped for and evidence of things not seen.

Heb. 1:1

This scripture passage stuck with me throughout my son Robby's illness and has stayed with me ever since. These words were branded into my soul as I watched my younger son, Eric, shovel dirt on Robby's casket one dreary, wet January morning. There are many times when I contemplate our final days with Robby. It was so difficult to watch him die, and at the same time, I have never felt the presence of God so close or experienced such inner peace.

In March 1993, Robby was diagnosed with an inoperable brain tumor (brain stem glioma). It's a tumor that attacks the central nervous system. I couldn't believe it was possible. None of our three children were ever sick; they were all very happy, healthy, and active children, always on the go, athletic, and smart. Robby loved sports and the outdoors. He never missed a chance to head to the creek near our house to catch frogs with Eric and his best friend, Nathan. Once I remember walking into our family room just in time for Robby to show me his latest catch. Eleven little frogs and one toad jumping from his bucket. He was all boy. He got into his share of mischief, fought with his brother and sister, had a great sense of humor and a heart of gold. His illness just didn't seem possible.

When the doctors gave us the news, we just sat there stunned. I remember the doctor who had to tell us. When he was finished, he said, "I'm so sorry. You have a wonderful boy. You've done a nice job raising him." All I could think to myself was, *We aren't done yet. What does he mean? He's only nine.* Then more doctors came in. The story remained the same. Robby would live maybe nine months with treatment or six months without. We were told that new breakthroughs were being made every day. The longer Robby lived, the better the chance something would be discovered that could save his life.

So started the treatment process. First was a series of radiation treatments. For six weeks, twice a day, Robby went in for radiation. I'll never forget his determination. Except for the days when he felt particularly bad, Robby always asked us to drop him off at school after his morning treatment. We then picked him up for treatment in the afternoon. As the treatment process neared its conclusion, Robby continued to show signs of improvement. We were really encouraged. At the end of June 1993, Robby underwent an MRI (magnetic resonance imaging) to see what effect the treatment had on the tumor. The doctors said Robby's tumor had had the best response they had ever seen. Then came the waiting. There was nothing more to do at the time but wait and see how he continued to respond.

This time was wonderful. Robby was almost his old self again. Most of his symptoms were gone, and he was able to do many of the things that had become impossible, like riding a bike or playing basketball. I'll never forget the joy I felt watching him in the front driveway shooting hoops. I had my little boy back!

Unfortunately, our joy was to be short-lived. Near the end of summer, the symptoms began to reappear, a sign that the tumor was growing again. More radiation was out of the question. They had given him all his little body could tolerate. My husband, Scott, and I asked the doctor to look into all the alternatives across the country. The doctor found out that the National Institutes of Health (NIH) in Bethesda, Maryland, was having some success with an experimental drug. We took Robby to Maryland for treatment. The program required that we take him to NIH every three weeks for an experimental chemotherapy—three thousand miles from home. Short of a miracle, this appeared to be our last hope. Two months into the program, Robby underwent another MRI. The experimental chemo was not working, and Robby was removed from the program.

As the tumor progressed and treatment options were exhausted, the doctors told us to make Robby as comfortable as possible. There was nothing more they could offer. We converted our family room into a room for Robby. We didn't want him tucked away in some corner of the house. On December 4, 1993, we set up a hospital bed in the family room and tried to make it as pleasant and comfortable as possible. More than anything else, Robby wanted to live. He wanted to beat the tumor, and he was not ready to accept defeat. Each year, Scott and the kids always made their annual trek with their cousins and grandfather to get our Christmas tree. This year would be no different. Robby insisted on being part of it although he wasn't strong enough to go to the actual tree-cutting site. Yet, as weak and sick as he was, he went and did what he could. When they returned home, we placed the tree at the foot of his bed where we could all enjoy it.

We just took things day by day. We were surrounded by so much love. Robby's fourth-grade class, about twenty-five in all, came to the house and performed the Christmas program. They also made a beautiful quilt for him. Each classmate and the teacher made a square. On each square was their picture and a message of encouragement and love. Family and friends would come by and just spend time with him. Robby especially loved Legos, so some of his friends and his grandfather would come by and sit at his beside and build Lego sets.

Every day Robby begged us to try to find some sort of treatment. And every day Robby experienced the effects of the tumor growth. Day by day, the simplest tasks became more and more difficult. There

were times when Robby felt forsaken, perhaps not unlike Christ in his final moments before death on the
cross. As the tumor grew, it continued to attack his
central nervous system. He knew what he wanted to
do and say, but it all became so difficult. A few days
after the trip to get the Christmas tree, Robby lost his
ability to walk. I have never felt so helpless in all my
life. About this same time, he lost his ability to talk.
Robby was a fighter though. When he was in second
grade, his teacher taught the kids in the class sign
language. Robby remembered what he had learned.
He still had the use of his hands so he began to communicate in sign language. Marie, our oldest child,
had also learned sign language and was able to communicate with Robby. She was also able to quickly
teach us some basics.

How do you comfort a child in this situation? All
their lives, children see their parents as the ones with
the answer, the solutions, the protection. We couldn't
give Robby any of those things. He would ask questions for which we didn't have answers. When our
priest came to the house and began to talk about
heaven, Robby just turned his head away. He didn't
want to hear any of that. He only wanted answers for
living. One day, a nun from hospice came to the
house to see Robby. She brought a little book called
A Letter to a Child with Cancer by Elisabeth Kübler-
Ross. The first time the nun read it to Robby, he just
turned his head. The next time she came to the house
and read the story, he signaled to her to read it again.
When she left, Robby asked me to read it over and
over. Robby was beginning to accept God's will and
the possibility of death.

Christmas came and went. It still remains pretty

much a blur. We really didn't think that Robby would live long enough to see Christmas that year. On December 26, a friend stopped by to see Robby. Knowing how much he loved the Seattle Mariners baseball team, our friend Bob told Robby that two Mariners were going to be in town on January 6. Bob was trying to arrange it so they would stop by the house to visit Robby. At first I thought there was no chance of Robby making it that long. Then I looked into his eyes and knew he was determined to see two members of his favorite team.

I had prayed that Robby would know that he would not be alone. His greatest fear in dying was the thought of being alone. I prayed and prayed for a sign. I needed God to let me know that Robby knew he would never be alone. One evening while I was helping Robby, he had the most beautiful, radiant smile on his face. I knew this was God's way of answering my prayer because Robby had not been able to move any facial muscles for several weeks. In the days that followed, Robby began looking around the room as if he was following something with his eyes. This continued for a couple of days, so finally I asked him if he saw something that I couldn't see and he nodded yes. I asked him if they were angels from heaven, and again, he nodded yes. One day as I saw Robby looking around the room, I asked him if he wanted to go with them—and he nodded yes. God in his infinite mercy had sent his messengers to comfort Robby. It was January 6. That night Robby got his promised visit by the Seattle Mariner players. Early the next morning Robby died.

Throughout this whole ordeal, Scott and I prayed that God would grant our miracle. We also prayed that if Robby wasn't cured, God would give us the strength and courage to accept God's answer to our prayers. Robby's faith astounded me. It was so pure, so absolute. Robby definitely wanted to live, but he was also very confident in his belief.

We were fortunate in the sense that Robby did not spend a lot of time in the hospital. We were very clear with all of the doctors from the outset. No matter what happened, Robby was only to be in the hospital when absolutely necessary. If it was something that could be done at home, that's where he would be.

Shortly after Robby's diagnosis, friends of ours organized a twenty-four-hour-prayer vigil. Over 100 people participated. That was just the beginning of the blessings. We never saw such a supportive community as we endured our struggle and as we continue through the healing process. From the very day that Robby was diagnosed, family and friends were there with us. Scott and I had always prided ourselves on being pretty self-reliant. When we were presented with this very difficult situation, we had some choices to make. We could withdraw and refuse the love and support of our community or we could allow it in to share in the journey and maybe help us find a purpose for all that was happening. We chose the latter. We needed the support. The support came from everywhere—our family, friends, neighbors, places of work, school, church, and loving members of the community. Schools in the community and from around the country sent letters to Robby. We were overwhelmed by the love, by the grace. We drew strength from the prayers and love.

Six months after Robby's death, while I was on my way to work, I was overcome by grief. I missed him so much. I wanted to turn around and go home, but I felt compelled to keep going. I was so depressed; my heart just ached. I parked my car in the parking structure about three blocks from my office (and thirteen miles from my home) and started toward the building. As I approached the sidewalk in front of the parking structure, I noticed on the sidewalk one of the ribbons (in Mariner colors) we had made for people to wear at Robby's funeral. As I reached down to pick it up. I was overcome with the realization that Robby is always with us. This was his way of letting me know that he was OK. That ribbon hangs in my office as a constant reminder of God's grace and mercy.

I know now that when we approach death and especially when someone we love approaches death we are all part of the journey. If allowed, God's grace and mercy will transcend the fear. It is not something to be avoided or tampered with. As much as I miss Robby, I draw comfort in knowing one day our family will be reunited again.

On January 5, 1994, the evening before Robby died, a good friend of mine came over to help me. When she returned home, she wrote the following poem. When I asked her what inspired her to write it, she simply said, "I wrote what I saw."

GOING HOME
He sees the things
that we cannot
For he is on his way

his eyes say words
our hearts can hear
"I'll meet the Lord today."

DEATH AS A HEALING EXPERIENCE

With His grace
and love for us
the Lord has sent a guide.

to gently urge him
on his way
to rest at Jesus' side.

God touched his heart
so long ago
and now He calls his name

"Come live with me
In my Father's house
where none are weak or lame."

She whispers go
as angels wait
his mother takes his hand
and places him in Mary's care
the Mother of the Lamb.

—M. Buckley, January 5, 1994

The following story is by Loreen Dawson about her husband, Dennis, who died from Hodgkin's disease. We pray that Dennis's angel may greet you, too, when your time has come.

Loreen:
As I write this, I realize it has been four years since my husband, Dennis, died. Sometimes it feels like a long, sad movie I watched once in a faraway place. Other times it feels like it's all still happening.

The pain is just as fresh, and the ache in my heart just as deep. You never really get over losing someone you love; you just learn to go on living without them.

Dennis was diagnosed with Hodgkin's disease in April of 1991. I remember when the doctor told us. We sat in those straight-backed doctor chairs separated from him by a huge wood desk. We didn't understand at first. What was Hodgkin's disease? Cancer! The world spun. We felt sick, confused, shocked. But he's too young, too healthy. How can he have cancer?

Despite the absence of signs and symptoms, the cancer was widely spread and had metastasized to his lungs and spleen. The odds weren't good. He had the standard chemotherapy protocol, which seemed to work for a while, then didn't.

He was offered a bone marrow transplant as "his only hope." It was indescribably horrible. Preparations took almost a month, then continuous megadoses of chemotherapy, radiation treatments that left horrendously painful burns inside his throat, constant vomiting, IV feedings, and daily tests.

The day the bone marrow is injected into a patient is called day 0—the first day of your new life. By day 7 there were signs that the bone marrow was beginning to grow. By day 30 there were signs that the cancer was, too. All that pain and suffering for nothing.

A few days later, Dennis begged me to take him out of the hospital and promise that I would never take him back. I kept that promise. I was scared that I wouldn't be able to look after him at home but also secretly relieved. I knew Dennis was tired of the constant intrusions and endless poking and prodding by more doctors and Med students than either of us could keep track of.

I had never seen anyone die before, never seen anyone really sick either. But I saw lots of both on the bone marrow transplant ward. Dennis had seen it, too. The younger patients were rushed up to the intensive care unit for their last few days—spent on morphine, with tubes stuck down their throats and IVs dripping into their veins, in last-ditch efforts to save or extend life. The older patients were left to die in their rooms, busy nurses doing their best to keep them comfortable, families standing awkwardly in the hall.

How did it feel, I wondered, to have to walk down that hall after your loved one has died? To take the elevator down seven floors, to walk down another long hall and across the parking lot until you were finally in the privacy of your own car. How did you drive home afterward? I started eyeing my fellow elevator passengers. How did you behave in the elevator after a death?

Dennis left the hospital unable to eat more than a mouthful at a time without vomiting, in constant pain, and with a broken spirit. His oncologist offered him palliative chemotherapy, but he refused. He wanted no more drugs and no more hospitals. I had no idea what to do to help him.

A neighbor suggested we see a naturopath. I was skeptical, but Dennis wanted to go. It changed his life and mine. He gave us things to do—hydrotherapy, diet changes, and supplements. He did physical therapy on Dennis and talked to him about his feelings, expectations, family, hopes, and dreams. Dennis started to eat, to hold down food, and to gain a few pounds. The constant pain he had experienced while in the hospital went away. He became calmer and more peaceful. The cancer progressed, but Dennis began to heal.

One day, out of the blue, Dennis announced he wanted to go to the coast "to see the ocean one last time." The coast was fifteen hundred miles away. The naturopath, the oncologist, and the nurses at the clinic where Dennis got blood transfusions all OK'd the trip. No one told me how sick he really was or how close he was to death. When I look back at a few pictures taken around then, I can't believe how blind I was, how I couldn't see it, but I didn't. Off we flew. To the coast. Vancouver.

We were in the air, somewhere over the prairies. Dennis kept staring out the window. "Who's that woman?" he asked. "You mean you see the form of a woman in the clouds?" I asked. "No," he said, "I see a woman out there, in those clouds." I looked but didn't see anything. I told he should get some sleep. My God, I thought, he's losing his mind.

A couple mornings later, Dennis's feet were so swollen he couldn't put on his shoes. I called an oncologist whose name we had been given to request a diuretic. He said to come right down. When we arrived, the nurse took one look at Dennis and ushered us immediately into an examining room even though the waiting room was packed. The doctor told me Dennis was dying. Yes, I knew that eventually he would die. "No," the doctor said. "He is dying right now."

I was shocked. I hadn't noticed he was so sick. When I looked at him, all I saw was the same man I had fallen in love with eight years earlier, perhaps with less hair, but the same beautiful brown eyes. Why hadn't anyone told me, really told me, before we left Winnipeg?

The doctor offered Dennis a palliative care room at the hospital. He refused. He wanted to die at home, but the doctor told him he would never make the flight back to Winnipeg. We phoned my parents in Victoria—a twenty-minute flight away. Of course, we could come over.

Before we left the office, the doctor pulled me aside and gave me a huge bottle of morphine. "Give him as much as he wants," he told me. Perhaps he couldn't imagine death without pain, but Dennis didn't need it.

The flight to Victoria was a nightmare. The airport was packed. I was on automatic pilot. Dennis seemed confused. There were no seats on the plane. We had to wait for two hours (and four flights) before we got on a flight.

By the time we arrived in Victoria, Mom had set everything up at home. Kim, a friend who is a nurse, had come over with supplies she thought we might need. By coincidence (if there is such a thing), the naturopath we had been seeing in Winnipeg was in Victoria visiting his brother. We called him. We were anxious and unsure of what to do. He came over the next morning and talked to us and the whole family. He told us what we would need to do and what we could expect.

Dennis spent the next day calling people to say good-bye. He slept a lot, and when he woke up, he kept talking about this woman he could see. I didn't understand at all: he seemed so lucid otherwise, and he wasn't taking any medication. I told the naturopath I thought he was having hallucinations. Dr. Turner encouraged me to ask him questions about what he was seeing and hearing. It was fascinating. I later read surprisingly similar accounts in a book about near-death experiences.

Dennis's breathing was starting to become more labored. He slept a lot and sweated so much that crystals formed on his skin. We had to change his sheets and T-shirt every couple hours and give him frequent sponge baths.

The next afternoon, Dennis asked for the phone. He wanted to talk to Dr. Turner. He told him he thought he would go first thing in the morning. I was very surprised to hear him say so but immediately felt more relaxed. I stopped worrying that every breath would be his last. Dennis liked to do things first thing in the morning, and he always did what he said he would.

Later he indicated that the woman was in the room. He could hear birds, too. I told him many times that it was OK for him to go and that I would be fine. I suggested he go with her and see what she wanted. He closed his eyes. When he opened them, some time later, he had the most incredible look of rapture, peace, and joy on his face. I had never seen him look so happy. I asked if he had seen where he was going. "Yes, beautiful" was all he said. In that moment, I realized that whatever lay on the other side would be far better for him than where he was now.

My parents and some friends came in to see him. They told him that I would be all right, that they would look after me. The priest arrived and administered the last rights.

Evening came, and we lit a candle in his room and put on a tape of his favorite music, which he had made for my mom the year before—mostly Liona Boyd classical guitar music. We drifted in and out of sleep. Around midnight, I got up to change his sheets—soaked again. I helped him sit up and pulled off his T-shirt. He stood up and walked two steps with a sheet wrapped around him and sat down in the armchair. He said he didn't want to go back to bed.

I sat beside him and waited. Mom or Kim would come in every couple of hours to check on us or just sit with us for a bit. I noticed that his body was getting very cold except for his face and chest and the hand I was holding. We drifted a little, the candle burned down, the music played.

We awakened as the first light appeared in the sky. The curtains were wide open, and Dennis's chair was facing the window. The sun began to rise over the horizon. He motioned that he couldn't see the sun.

I told him it was OK to go, that I would be all right, and that my family would look after me. I asked him if the woman was there; he nodded. I told him if he wanted to see the sunrise, he would have to leave now and go with her. He looked at me, then his eyes closed. One last breath and then he just stopped breathing. No pain, no struggle.

I sat there stunned. It was over. Suddenly, I saw silver sparkles rising out of his body. They hovered for a moment, then disappeared out the window. I went to the window and looked out. Flying past the window were three large black birds. Two flew smoothly and easily ahead, while the third seemed to be struggling to keep up, its wings flapping erratically. They were flying toward the sunrise.

The death of Dennis was not just the tragic loss of an intelligent, handsome, caring young man long before anyone was ready to let him go. It was also the loss of children dreamed of but never conceived, of plans made and never carried out, of nieces and nephews who will never know what a wonderful man their uncle was, of a son who will never again visit the home farm, of a brother missing from the Sunday table. It is the loss of the special things of everyday life.

And yet, although it's hard to admit, much was also gained. Horizons were opened for me that I could not even have dreamed of in my previous life. My mind and heart have been expanded in ways I would never have imagined was possible.

I am no longer afraid of death. Death is nothing more than a shifting from this life to the next. I have seen it with my own eyes and felt it with my heart. In the words of Richard Bach, "What the caterpillar calls the end of the world, The Master calls the Butterfly."

We introduced you to Alexandra Ellis and her parents earlier. Her complete story, as told by her parents, follows as our final story. The story of her courage and humanity is especially close to our hearts. Alexandra's beautiful spirit often whispered to us as we wrote this book.

Cliff and Regina Ellis:
ALEXANDRA THE BRAVE

When our daughter Alexandra was three and one-half years old, we learned she had cancer. We had unanswerable questions and experienced unthinkable terror as we confronted the responses of medical technology with all its severe treatments and protocols.

All we wanted was a cure; all we wanted was our baby back; all we wanted was a healing.

All of us began fighting for her life: the doctors, the nurses, our friends, our family . . . but Alexandra did the hardest work. For two years, Alex took lots of medicine, had days and days of chemotherapy (six days straight every three weeks for fifteen months), took many, many vitamins, and herbal tinctures. She took medications in the mornings, during the days, and through the nights. There were pills to swallow, pills to chew, liquids to drink, medicine in needles, medicine through tubes, chemo in her catheter, chemo in IVs, and medicine with pumps.

In her own words, "Taking so much medicine is a real pain in the butt." She said it was hard to always have to take medicine and undergo chemo when she felt so bad. We listened, we cried. We wanted it to stop. But we kept working, kept fighting. We gave her as many choices as we could think of: which medicine, which minute, which flavor.

When Alexandra began chemotherapy, doctors told us she might not live through the toxic treatment. We sat down to think: if all we have is thirty, sixty, ninety days left together, how do we want to spend them? What do we want to do? How are we going to heal ourselves during this challenge?

We talked a lot, we cried, we mourned the normal life we were about to leave behind. We made lists, we cried again and thought about our daughter, our family, and what we are all about. We decided to make a To Live List. We put things on it: play more; sing out loud more; go camping in the backyard—just because; keep laughing; acknowledge our struggle and how different our lives will be from all our friends; be honest;

keep advocating for Alex and empowering her; and reach out to help others. Alex included things like go to Disneyland again, keep going to preschool, have more tea parties, and go barefoot at the beach even in the winter. We tried to do as much living as we could. We knew that all the time we could count on was right then. Looking back, it is clear: we had begun our healing.

Alex enjoyed keeping track of things: of chemo days, pokes with a needle, hard-to-take meds, bone scans, CAT scans, bone marrow aspirations, and all of these things happened a lot. We kept a tally of the really hard things, and Alexandra earned credits at the Disney Store. After she felt well enough, we went shopping. I'm pretty sure the Disney Store employees knew when Alex had had a hard week. Even when Alex was dying, she still kept track. When she no longer was able to make the trip, her nonna and I would do the shopping. "No clothes, Mom," she whispered, laboring just to breathe. "Only the toys!"

Because Alex had cancer, our family met a lot of exceptional people. We met many doctors who worked hard to make the cancer abate. We met nurses who with their humor and tenderness took great care of Alex. We met many other people with cancer and many families who have a child with cancer. We met lots of other people who wanted to help us—to listen, to play, to be our friends. They are exceptional and have helped us heal along the way. They have told us that they too have healed through Alexandra's struggle.

When Alex was diagnosed, our incredible family and our unbelievable friends quickly rallied around us and held each of us—Cliff, Zachary, Alexandra, and me. We have continually felt their presence, their love, and their deep compassion as we journeyed into the unknown, with its darkness and pain. In fact, when our family and friends united to support us, it was like the Time–Warner or Bell–AT&T mergers: they planned, organized, divided tasks, and scheduled. They conference-called, E-mailed, and earnestly, lovingly, and unbelievably accomplished wonders, amazing feats, and miracles for our family during this crisis.

During our last round of chemo, Alex's cancer relapsed. We had two options: a bone marrow transplant with only a 10 percent survival rate at two years and the real possibility of her dying during or after the procedure or go home and really live the rest of Alexandra's life. It was a crossroads, a tortuous, agonizing decision; we ultimately gave Alex the choice and explained the transplant. She said, "I'm tired of the hospital, Mom and Daddy. No more chemo!" She said that what she really wanted to do was go to Hawaii and swim with the dolphins. We left the hospital for the last time—Alexandra had finished all the treatment her body could withstand. Traditional and nontraditional medicine had given us all they had to offer. It was now, as we moved toward our daughter's death, that we began to struggle every moment, searching for ways to heal. It was only by embracing our love for one another, the choices that we made, and the struggle to maintain the quality of life, even during treatment, that we attained healing, however pained or brief.

Our family and a few friends organized a three-week trip to Hawaii, with everything donated by an incredible woman and some of her friends (airfare, condo, spending money, rides on a helicopter, a horse, a whale-watching boat, and submarine voyage 130 feet deep). We arranged for Alex to swim and play with two dolphins in a private lagoon with their trainer. She fed them, she touched them, she loved them, and it was one of the most treasured memories of her life.

While we were in Hawaii, friends and family also designed sixty-five individual handmade squares for a special quilt for Alex. A few of them worked all day and all night to get it to us before Alex died so that we could wrap its loving energy around her.

We are amazed and forever thankful to our loving family and friends who have given us many memories, much help, and made many of our dreams come true in Alexandra's lifetime. I once read that the power of love is found in the circle of family. Our circle of family has grown to include so many who have given a piece of their heart to Alex and to my husband, Cliff; my son, Zachary; and myself.

Having a child with cancer makes life so very hard. Many times we felt like we were adrift in an ocean amidst a raging typhoon, hanging on for our sanity, for our family, for a cure, for healing. Most importantly, Alexandra taught us that healing can happen even when there is no cure. She showed us that healing includes every aspect of our being—our emotions, our souls, our spirits, our thoughts, our actions, our words, and our love. She knew that healing our tired bodies and broken hearts would take hard work involving all of the people who deeply loved and cared about her.

When Alex was dying at home and laboring so hard to breathe, she lay in our bed with candlelight

and soft music. Many of her friends and five generations of her family visited her. They sat next to her,
read books, sang songs, told stories, talked to her, gave
her peppermint lotion foot rubs, combed her hair,
cried, and just lay quietly and held her. When her
hands and body did not work, we moved her arms so
she could still touch and caress her favorite cat,
Simba, who kept a vigil on the bed until Alex died.

Two nights before Alex died, she was in a coma,
and Cliff and I stayed with her all through the night,
whispering secrets, telling stories, singing her favorite
songs, crying and laughing and letting go of our first-
born, beautiful blue-eyed girl-child. These were the
hardest days, the most physically and emotionally demanding. We stayed awake with her every moment;
our bodies raged with extreme exhaustion, our minds
screamed in turmoil as we helplessly watched her
struggle to breathe, her chest heaving for endless minutes in these forty-eight hours, her body rapidly losing
control. Yet, without her voice, without a movement,
without a look from her sparkling eyes, Alex showed
us that for our family, our healing was happening in
the miracle of her death.

The day before she died, we gave her a warm bath,
oxygen tubes and all, and soothed her tired body and
our broken hearts. We helped her out of this world
just as we'd welcomed her into it as an infant, by
cuddling her close, whispering loving words in a safe,
warm bath. We spoke to her of the dolphins she swam
with in Hawaii. We told her that when she died she
could always come back home to us whenever she
wanted and crawl into our beds, ease into our laps on
the rocking chair, and play with her little brother,
Zachary, in his room.

On Sunday morning, Alex waited for Zachary to come home, crawl up onto the bed, tell her he loved her, and say good-bye. Minutes later, Cliff and I were at her side as she took her last breaths and effortlessly stopped breathing. It was then we felt her beautiful spirit slip out of its listless cocoon. Our beautiful little angel soared free from the pain and suffering.

With courage and love, Alexandra Rene Rathburn Ellis valiantly won her long battle with cancer and peacefully died May 7, 1995, at 9:30 A.M. She was five and a half years old.

Alexandra's death has left a space in our hearts, our home, our lives. But her courage—through her illness and through her death—has taught us how to heal. Now it is we who face a challenge: to comfort each other, to rebuild our lives, to use the lessons we learned in her struggle with cancer, and to live better lives because of Alexandra. We will always love you, our sweet Alexandra, and we will always miss you.

Jan:

I was privileged to serve as a midwife to Regina at the birth of her third child, Kathleen Alexandra. It had been only nine months since I had served as a midwife to her daughter Alexandra during her dying time. The parallels of birth and death were poignantly illustrated to me through this experience.

The labor and delivery were filled with a variety of emotions. Memories of Alexandra's death were still so fresh. Regina and Cliff worked as an incredible team. As I watched them it took me back to when they were caring for Alexandra during her final days. There was a combined strength and natural flow to every action taken. As Regina's contractions grew in intensity, Cliff guided her through them. Family and friends gathered as the birth drew nearer.

When Kathleen Alexandra was born she was wrapped in the same angel blanket that her sister Alexandra had been wrapped in at her death. Gathered around the baby were the same family and friends that had surrounded Alexandra during her dying time. Each of us present at this birth were reminded of the cycle of life. Our tears were a response to the joyfulness of birth and the sorrow of wishing Alexandra could be here to share in it.

As I held baby Kathleen in her pretty pink hat, I felt her sister Alexandra's Angel spirit. I imagine she was giving her angel kisses and telling her how pretty her pink hat was. Alexandra loved pink!

We hope that this book has helped to illuminate the natural process of dying that occurs in our final weeks and days. We pray that you may remember that there is always hope, love, and time for all that you need. May you live fully in the time that is given to you.

Appendix A: References

"All About . . . Hospice House." 1990. Portland, Ore.: Hospice House, Inc.

Amenta, M., and N. Bohenet. 1986. *Nursing Care of the Terminally Ill*. Boston/Toronto: Little, Brown.

Anderson, Joan Webster. 1992. *Where Angels Walk: True Stories of Heavenly Visitors*. Guidepost edition. Carmel, N.Y.: Barton & Brett.

Aries, Philipps. 1981. *The Hour of Our Death*. New York: Knopf.

Bach, R. 1970. *Jonathan Livingston Seagull*. New York: Macmillan.

Beck, Renee, and Sydney Merrick. 1990. *The Art of Ritual*. Berkeley, Calif.: Celestial Arts.

Beresford, Larry. 1993. *The Hospice Handbook: A Complete Guide*. Boston: Little, Brown.

Boyle, W., and A. Saine. 1988. *Lecture in Naturopathic Hydrotherapy*. East Palestine, Ohio: Buckeye Naturopathic Press.

Chase, Marilyn. 1995. "Gently Guiding the Gravely Ill to the

APPENDIX A: REFERENCES

End'' (Health Journal). *Wall Street Journal,* February 27, 1995, section B, page 1.

Clarke, Peter B. 1993. *The World's Religions.* Pleasantville, N.Y.: Reader's Digest Association.

Clay, Rotha Mary. 1966. *The Medieval Hospitals of England.* Frank Cass.

Cohen, Kenneth P. 1979. *Hospice Prescription for Terminal Care.* Germantown, Md.: Aspen Systems Corp.

Cunningham, Frank J. (Ed.). 1983. *Words to Love By . . . Mother Teresa.* Notre Dame, Ind.: Ave Maria Press.

Doyle, D.; G. Hanks; and N. MacDonald. 1993. *Oxford Textbook of Palliative Medicine.* Oxford: Oxford University Press.

DuBoulay, S. 1984. *Cicely Saunders, The Founder of the Modern Hospice Movement.* London: Hodder & Stoughton.

Feldman, C., and J. Kornfield. 1991. *Stories of the Spirit of the Heart.* San Francisco: Harper San Francisco.

Foos-Graber, Anya. 1989. *Deathing.* York Beach. Maine: Nicholas-Harp.

Gaskin, I. 1978. *Spiritual Midwifery.* Summertown, Tenn.: The Book Publishing Company.

Haber, Judith; Anita M. Leach; Sylvia Schudy; and Barbara Flynn Sideleau. 1982. *Comprehensive Psychiatric Nursing.* New York: McGraw-Hill.

Ingerman, Sandra. 1993. *Welcome Home: Following Your Soul's Journey Home.* San Francisco: Harper San Francisco.

Irving, Janis. 1974. ''Vigilance and Decision Making in a Personal Crisis.'' G. Cochlo et al. *Coping and Adaptation.* New York: Basic Books.

Kaminski, P., and R. Katz. 1994. *Flower Essence Repertory.* Nevada City, Calif.: Flower Essence Society.

Karma-glin-pa. 1972. *The Tibetan Book of the Dead.* Mount Vernon, N.Y.: Peter Pauper Press.

Kaye, P. 1989. *Notes on Symptom Control in Hospice and Palliative Care.* Essex, Conn.: Hospice Education Institute.

Kübler-Ross, E. 1970. *On Death and Dying.* New York: Macmillan.

——. 1979. *A Letter to a Child with Cancer.* Head Waters, Va.

Levine, S. 1979. *A Gradual Awakening.* New York: Doubleday.

——. 1984. *Who Dies? An Investigation of Conscious Living and*

Conscious Dying. Garden City, N.Y.: Anchor Press/ Doubleday.

McCaffrey, M., and A. Beebe. 1989. *Pain Clinical Management for Nursing Practice.* St. Louis: Mosby.

Mitchell, Stephen. 1987. *Tao Te Ching.* New York: Harper & Row.

Munley, Anne. 1983. *The Hospice Alternative: A New Context for Death and Dying.* New York: Basic Books.

National Hospice Organization. 1994–1995. *Guide to the Nation's Hospices.* Arlington, Va.

Olds, Sally B.; Marcia L. Condon; Patricia A. Ladewig; and Sharon V. Davidson. 1980. *Obstetric Nursing.* Menlo Park, Calif.: Addison-Wesley.

Oregon Health Decisions/Oregon Hospice Association. 1994. A Report of the August 11, 1994, Community Meetings. "Request for Physician-Assisted Death: How Will You Vote?" Portland, Ore.: Oregon Health Decisions.

Pinto, Santan. 1993. *Prayer in Your Life.* Seattle, Wash.

Rinpoche, Sogyal. 1992. *The Tibetan Book of Living and Dying.* San Francisco: Harper San Francisco.

Saunders, C. 1969. "The Moment of Truth: Care of the Dying Person." In L. Pearson (Ed.), *Death & Dying,* pp. 49–78). Cleveland: Western Reserve University Press.

Schneider, M., and J. Bernard. 1992. *Midwives to the Dying.* Portland, Ore.: Angels' Work.

Schneider, Miriam. Fall 1992. Hospice Nurtures Hope and Healing." *Friends of VNA Hospice Newsletter,* Vol. 1, No. 5. Portland, Ore.: Visiting Nurse Association.

Schucman, Helen. 1976. *A Course in Miracles.* Tiburon, Calif.: Foundation for Inner Peace.

Seward, Desmond. 1996. *The Monks of War.* London: Viking Penguin.

Siegel, Bernie 1993. *How to Live between Office Visits.* New York: HarperCollins.

———. 1986. *Love, Medicine & Miracles.* New York: Harper Perennial.

Sire, H.J.A. 1994. *The Knights of Malta.* New Haven: Yale University Press.

Spiegel, David. 1993. *Living Beyond Limits. New Hope and Help For Facing Life-Threatening Illness.* New York: Times Books.

APPENDIX A: REFERENCES

Stoddard, S. 1978. *The Hospice Movement: A Better Way of Caring for the Dying.* New York: Stein & Day.

Travelbee, J. 1977. *Interpersonal Aspects of Nursing.* Philadelphia: Davis.

Williams, Terry Tempest. 1991. *Refuge: An Unnatural History of Family and Place.* New York: Random House.

Appendix B:
Resources

Reading List

The process of facing a life-challenging illness can be full of fear, confusing, and lonely. With support, it can also be life changing and transforming. The purpose of this reading list is to provide you with some support and resources to assist you and your loved ones on this journey.

Cancer and AIDS

Alpha Institute. *The Alpha Book on Cancer and Living.* The Alpha Institute, Alameda, Calif., 1993.

Austin, S., and C. Hitchcock. *Breast Cancer.* Prima Publishing, Ricklin, Calif., 1994.

Kübler-Ross, E. *AIDS: The Ultimate Challenge.* Macmillan, London/Collier Macmillan, New York, N.Y., 1987.

APPENDIX B: RESOURCES

Children's Books for Ages 1 to 110

Boulder, Jim. *Saying Goodbye—A Coloring Book*. Santa Rosa, Calif., 1989.

Jampolsky, Gerald. *There Is a Rainbow Behind Every Dark Cloud*. Berkeley, Calif., 1978.

Kübler-Ross, Elisabeth. *A Letter to a Child with Cancer*. Head Waters, Va., 1979.

Kübler-Ross, Elisabeth. *Remember the Secret*. Celestial Arts, Berkeley, Calif., 1982.

Sanford, Doris. *In Our Neighborhood David Has AIDS*. Multnomah Press, Portland, Ore., 1989.

Sanford, Doris. *It Must Hurt a Lot—A Child's Book about Death*. Multnomah Press, Portland, Ore., 1986.

Grief

Beck, R., and S. Metricks. *The Art of Ritual*. Celestial Arts, Berkeley, Calif., 1990.

Berkus, R. *To Heal Again Towards Serenity and the Resolution of Grief*. Red Rose Press, Los Angeles, 1984.

Livingston, Gordon. *Only Spring and Mourning the Death of My Son*. Harper San Francisco, San Francisco, 1995.

Osmont, K. *What Can I Say? How to Help Someone Who Is Grieving, A Guide*. Nobility Press, Portland, Ore., 1988.

Tatelbaum, J. *The Courage to Grieve: Creative Living, Recovery, and Growth Through Grief*. Harper & Row, New York, 1980.

Healing of the Body and Spirit

Feldman, C., and J. Kornfield. *Stories of the Spirit of the Heart*. Harper San Francisco, San Francisco, 1991.

Jampolsky, G. *Out of Darkness into the Light—The Journey of Inner Healing*. Bantam, New York, 1989.

Krieger, D. *The Therapeutic Touch*. Prentice-Hall, Englewood Cliffs, N.J., 1979.

Siegel, B. *How to Live Between Office Visits*. Harper Collins, New York, 1993.

Siegel, B. *Peace, Love & Healing*. Harper Perennial, New York, 1993.

Siegel, B. *Love, Medicine & Miracles*. Harper Perennial, New York, 1986.

Simonton, Carl, and Stephanie Simonton. *Getting Well Again*. Bantam, New York, 1978.

Journey of Death and Dying

Carroll, D. *Living with Dying*. Paragon House, New York.

Foos-Graber, Anya. *Deathing*. Nicholas-Harp, York Beach, Maine, 1989.

Kübler-Ross, Elisabeth. *On Death and Dying*. Macmillan, New York, 1969.

Levine, S. *Who Dies? An Investigation of Conscious Living and Conscious Dying*. Anchor Press/Doubleday, Garden City, N.Y., 1982.

Riemer, Jack. *Jewish Reflections on Death*. Schocken Books, 1987.

Sogyal, Rinpoche. *The Tibetan Book of Living and Dying*. Harper San Francisco, San Francisco, 1992.

Personal Experiences of Living and Dying— A Life-Challenging Illness

Brinker, N. *The Race Is One Step at a Time*. Simon & Schuster, New York, 1990.

Cousins, Norman. *Anatomy of an Illness as Perceived by the Patient*. Norton, New York, 1979, Bantam, New York, 1981.

Kübler-Ross, E. *To Live Until We Say Goodbye*. Prentice-Hall, Englewood Cliffs, N.J., 1978.

Wilber, K. *Grace and Grit*. Shambhala Publications, Boston, 1991.

Williams, Terry Tempest, *Refuge: An Unnatural History of Family and Place*. Random House, New York, 1991.

APPENDIX B: RESOURCES

Spirituality

Burnham, S. *A Book of Angels.* Ballantine, New York, 1990.
Goodwin, M. *Angels, an Endangered Species.* Simon & Schuster, New York, 1990.
Harlow, R. "The Day We Saw Angels." Guideposts, December 1986, pp. 24–27.
Savary, L., and P. Berne. *Kything: The Art of Spiritual Presence.* Paulist Press, New York, Mahwah, N.J., 1988.
Schucman, Helen. *A Course in Miracles.* Foundation for Inner Peace, Tiburon, Calif., 1976.

Visualization and Meditation

Epstein, G. *Healing Visualizations Creating Health Through Imagery.* Bantam, New York, 1989.
Gawain, S. *Creative Visualization.* Whatever Publishing, Mill Valley, Calif., 1978.
Levine, S. *A Gradual Awakening.* Doubleday, New York, 1979.
Swirsky, Michael. *At the Threshold: Jewish Meditations on Death.* Jason Aronson, Northvale, New Jersey, 1996.

Organizations

Alexandra Ellis Memorial Childrens Cancer Association
P.O. Box 19734
Portland, OR 97219

American Cancer Society
159 Clifton Road NE
Atlanta, GA 30329

Association for Death Education and Counseling
2211 Arthur Avenue
Lakewood, OH 44107

Children's Hospice International
(703)684-0330

Compassionate Friends, Inc.
P.O. Box 3696
Oak Brook, IL 60522-3696
(312)990-0010

ECaP (Exceptional Cancer Patients)
1302 Chapel Street
New Haven, CT 06511
(203)865-8392

Elisabeth Kübler-Ross
Shanti Nilaya
South Route 616
Head Waters, VA 24442
(703)396-3441

Haneman Foundation
Stephen and Andrea Levine
P.O. Box 100
Chamisal, NM 87521

National Hospice Organization
1901 North Moore Street
Suite 901
Arlington, VA 22209
(703)243-5900

Shanti Project
525 Howard Street
San Francisco, CA 94105
(415) 777-2273

Stephens Ministries
1325 Boland Street
St. Louis, MO 63117
(314) 645-5511

APPENDIX B: RESOURCES

Locally you can find support through the following:
- Bereavement counseling and support groups.
- Church organizations.
- Home health departments and hospice care teams.
- The local health department in your county.
- Your health care team.

Angels' Work

We have a business partnership called Angels' Work. Our goal is to provide support and guidance for those experiencing loss from illness or the death and dying process. We offer the following support services:
- An interactive workshop presentation entitled "Serving As Midwives to the Dying."
- Speaker presentations to health care professionals, service organizations, or others interested in exploring dying as a natural life event.
- Support group leadership.
- Individual or family consultations.

Please inquire at:
Angels' Work
P.O. Box 994
Sherwood, OR 97140
(503)795-7000

E-mail address:
AngelsWk@aol.com

Index

INDEX

233

INDEX